D0429960

14.95
13.45

750

The Mother Knot

Jane Lazarre

Introduction by Maureen T. Reddy

DUKE UNIVERSITY PRESS
Durham and London 1997

This is a memoir. The names of some people

have been changed to protect their privacy.

© 1976 Jane Lazarre

This edition © 1997 Duke University Press

Originally published in 1976 by McGraw-Hill Book

Company; first published as a Beacon paperback in 1986.

All rights reserved

Printed in the United States of America on acid-free paper ∞

Typeset in Joanna by Keystone Typesetting, Inc.

Library of Congress Cataloging-in-Publication Data appear

on the last printed page of this book.

For Douglas Hughes White

Introduction

Maureen T. Reddy

Reading *The Mother Knot* more than twenty years after its first publication, I am struck by how contemporary this terrific book seems. The struggles that Jane Lazarre details—to hold on to her inner self while caught up in the exhausting, consuming work of mothering; to forge a new kind of relationship with her husband; to reconcile her past as a daughter with her present as a mother—are at once intensely individual and widely shared by new mothers. The kind of truth-telling about motherhood as a daily reality that Jane attempts with other mothers, and of which *The Mother Knot* is itself a triumphant example, continues to be rare indeed. Jane Lazarre remains one of the few writers to take as her central theme maternal subjectivity, a mother viewed from a maternal perspective, as opposed to a child's.

I originally read *The Mother Knot* when my first child was two years old and just beginning to sleep through the night reliably. My husband and I had recently moved from Minneapolis, where we had a large circle of friends, to a suburb outside Philadelphia, where we knew almost no one and where it sometimes seemed we would never know anyone, worn out as we were by the demands of new jobs and parenthood. Worse, I was so caught up in the minutiae of daily life with a toddler that I found it nearly impossible to carry on a fully "adult," nonparental discussion with the people I did meet. What I wanted to talk about—my son, incessantly, endlessly—seemed unlikely to hold much interest for anyone else; what *they* wanted to talk about often held little interest for me, although it would have fully absorbed me just two years earlier. And then a new friend, the feminist philosopher Sara Ruddick, threw me a lifeline in the form of Jane Lazarre's book, for which she had just written a new introduction.

I read *The Mother Knot* that first time greedily, hungrily, thrilled to find affirmation of my own ambivalence, my powerful love for my son, and my utter despair that I would ever be free of his demands again. Of her son Benjamin, Jane says to her friend Anna, "I would die for him. . . . All those movies about mothers running in front of trucks and bullets to save their children are true. I would much prefer to die than lose him. I guess that's love . . . but he has destroyed my life and I live only to find a way of getting it back again." Anna and Jane learn "to expect sentences to have two parts, the second seeming to contradict the first, the unity lying only in our growing ability to tolerate ambivalence—for that is what motherly love is like." Certainly that is what motherly love is like for Jane and for me as well; judging from the reactions of friends to whom I've since given *The Mother Knot* and from the few narratives about mothering since published, ambivalence is a defining feature of motherhood for many women, perhaps especially for feminists. But that ambivalence is nowhere to be found—in the 1970s or in the 1990s—in the "official" social discourse about mothering.

The Mother Knot's undatedness, its contemporary feel, arises in part from the stasis in that official discourse during the past two decades. Despite inroads into traditional family arrangements made by the feminist movement, increasing public consciousness of the comparatively small percentage of American families that fit the father-mother-two children (all of the same race) fantasy, and large numbers of families with small children in which the mother works outside the home, public discussions of motherhood have scarcely altered since 1976. Inevitably, these public discussions have profound effects on how women mother and on how they see their mothering work. The official line on mothering goes something like this: *good* mothers stay at home while their children are small, are perfectly content with staying at home with those children, are dedicated exclusively to their children's well-being, have boundless love for their children, never regret having children, never hit their children, never speak sharply to their children, arrange their lives around their children, including making household chores into games for the children and finding as many learning experiences for the children as possible every single day. And yet mothering is not fully valued, is still not seen as "real work"; hence, in some circles, mothers are also pressured to retain professional identities apart from mothering. "I mother" is not an acceptable answer to "what do you do?" Small wonder, given the powerful and constant social expectations

of mothers, that mothering tends to be a site of competition, not coop-
eration, for women. Further, the notion that good mothers want the
best for their children—with "the best" being as narrowly defined as
"good mothering"—exacerbates the competitiveness, dividing women
from each other and reducing the possibility of mothers banding together to work for the good of all children. Women who do not con-
form to the ideal are bad mothers; shame too often silences them or
forces them into lying.

In *The Mother Knot*, Jane first silences herself, shamed by the gulf between the official story on mothering and her own experience, then is
silenced by other mothers who are so threatened by the prospect of the
official story being a lie that they cannot bear to hear what Jane has to
say. Once, after a few particularly difficult nights with a wakeful, crying
Benjamin, Jane answers an acquaintance's rhetorical question about the
joys of motherhood by saying she feels motherhood is not wonderful
but "quite miserable and exhausting"; the other woman replies, "Oh,
don't say that." Eventually, however, Jane finds other mothers who are
willing to tell and to hear the truth, however painful it might be. While
she occasionally succumbs to the temptation to compete for "the prize
of Best Mother of the Year," she comes to realize that competition
"result[s] only in intensifying [her] loneliness" and determines to re-
sist. The comradeship of other mothers proves exhilarating and freeing;
I read it as contributing to Jane's eventual ability to insist—to her husband and, more importantly, to herself—on the space and the time to
write.

The truth, of course, is multiple and various. There is no one right
way to be a good mother and no single set of feelings appropriate to
motherhood. However obvious this may seem, it can be difficult to
remember in the face of overwhelming evidence that U.S. society sanc-
tions only a very narrow definition of good mothering. The dismissive
admonishment "don't say that" enforces that narrow definition by refusing to allow a different story to be told. Audre Lorde once noted that
it is not women's differences that divide us but our silence, our failure
to speak honestly about those differences. Although she was speaking
specifically of race, Lorde's point applies to the many differences about
which women need to speak. In *Maternal Thinking: Toward a Politics of Peace*,
Sara Ruddick points to *The Mother Knot* as an example of the maternal
stories she believes women need to share so that the experience of
motherhood can be understood and maternal thinking valued. We still

have too few of those stories, so I am delighted that Lazarre's wonderful book will be available to another generation of readers and will perhaps inspire other mothers to share their own maternal stories.

As Ruddick points out in her 1986 introduction to *The Mother Knot*, Jane is not Everywoman; that is, many elements of her experience are not at all "typical." Jane is a New Yorker, a Jewish intellectual, a daughter of dedicated communists, a feminist, a writer; statistically speaking, none of this is typical of American mothers. Furthermore, she is married to a man she loves and who loves her; they have money adequate for meeting all their needs and many of their wants; both are well-educated. I doubt these statements could be made with equal truth about most mothers. However, who exactly *is* typical when it comes to mothering? Perhaps two elements mark Jane most profoundly as atypical: her identity as a writer and her status as a white woman married to a black man.

Conventionally, mothering and writing have been seen as antagonistic, as irreconcilable pursuits; even writers who are themselves mothers have not usually written about motherhood itself. This convention has finally begun to erode, as many feminist writers have turned their attention to mothering in the past decade. Nonetheless, most mothers— like most non-mothers—are not writers. Jane explains that she has always kept "record books," writing about her thoughts and experiences: "For me, living without writing things down has always been confusing. I never feel as if I understand anything until it is described over and over at great length. Months or years later, after the time which has given me such great sadness or happiness or fear or pleasure is past, I sit down by myself and read over what I have written. Then I think, Oh, so that's what happened. I see now how I felt." Initially, mothering and writing do seem incompatible to Jane, beginning with pregnancy. Trying to revise a novel she has begun, Jane finds that the "task demanded discipline and attention, two abilities which were more and more retreating into the realms of memory." Not until several years later, when Benjamin is settled happily into a day-care center that his mother has helped to build, does Jane finally have decent periods of time in which she can attend seriously to writing. At that point, however, mothering ceases to be a barrier and actually becomes *enabling* for Jane as a writer. As readers, we realize that the book we are reading is one that Jane could not have written without the experience of mothering. Jane's voice gains strength as her story progresses, with the completed tale standing as a record of her journey toward becoming a narrating self, a writer. Further, by making sense of her story through writing, Jane is able to make a choice the result of which opens the book: she and her husband decide to have a second child, born as *The Mother Knot* begins. Mothering and writing thus intertwine.

To my knowledge, when *The Mother Knot* came out, it was the first book to describe an interracial marriage from the inside and to treat that relationship directly and without the assumption of pathology or tragedy that usually—even now—attends treatments of transracial love. Race first comes up in the book's second chapter. Jane has just learned that she is pregnant and is imagining how people will react to the news: "Then, in the moment of thinking about my baby's grandparents, I began to sense the complicated world which awaited my child. My father would be waiting for the Jewish intellectual his grandchild would surely be, the inheritor of generations of Old World culture and New World socialism, a member of the army fighting for social justice, a servant to the people, a traveler in the grandfather's footsteps. Meanwhile, my father-in-law would be expecting a Black warrior, surpassing James in athletic agility and academic achievement." At this moment, Jane's relationship to race changes dramatically. Until three years before, when she married James, Jane was simply a white woman, albeit one without full membership in "the American club," as she puts it, by virtue of her background as a child of Jewish Communists. Marrying James made her part of "a political entity: Black man married to white woman," a target of censorious remarks from both blacks and whites and privy to a perspective on racism few whites ever experience. As mother-to-be of a black child, Jane feels "a new anger" as she begins to imagine the struggles her child will face.

Although Jane occasionally thinks of Benjamin as a "hybrid"—a term less loaded with the ugliness of racist history than "mulatto," surely— she mostly thinks of him as black, when she thinks of his race at all. It is important to note that the struggles she envisions in his future have little to do with his being biracial or having a white mother, and virtually everything to do with his being black in a racist society. Benjamin is no "tragic mulatto" but a black child with a white mother. Interestingly, the few books written since by members of interracial families about their experiences—Hettie Jones's *How I Became Hettie Jones*, my own *Crossing the Color Line: Race, Parenting, and Culture*, and James McBride's *The Color of Water*, for instance—tend to confirm this perspective. Certainly

Jane Lazarre's two later books focusing on interracial families, the novel *Worlds Beyond My Control* and the recent memoir *Beyond the Whiteness of Whiteness*, suggest that biraciality is in itself something of a non-issue, as the child's struggles mirror those of other black people and the white parent must learn about racism from the perspective of racism's targets. Jane puts one significant lesson she learns this way: "There are a Black world and a white world and very rarely do these two overlap."

Ordinary racism becomes more visible to Jane as she identifies with her small son, which is not to say that she was ever unaware of racism, but that awareness of racism begins to occupy the forefront of her consciousness as opposed to being generally in the background. At the hospital after Benjamin's birth, nurses dub him "Little Black Panther." White neighbors in New Haven panic at the prospect of a demonstration in support of actual Black Panthers—Ericka Huggins and Bobby Seale, then imprisoned—and display their racist fantasies by devising a guard system to protect them against the (entirely imaginary) hordes of angry blacks they fear. Later, when searching for suitable day care, Jane can find no integrated centers. At one place she and Benjamin visit, Jane asks if there are any black children enrolled. "Oh, but you just missed one," comes the reply. "A lovely Black child, but bright and sweet like yours." Jane understands that unconscious racism lies beneath that second "but," a profound knowledge that forever separates her from the heedless privileges of whiteness.

Like Jane, I am a white woman married to a black man; again like Jane, I have found that my marriage made much less difference in my relation to race than did my becoming a mother of black children. When I first read *The Mother Knot*, I had been looking for two years for books about interracial families and had found none, or at least none that in any way approximated the life I was living. I found books about tragic love affairs between blacks and whites, such as Ann Petry's *The Narrows*; children's books about white families rejecting black children related to them by birth or adoption, and then learning the error of their ways and unlearning some of their racism; tirades against interracial romance by both black and white authors; and sociological studies purporting to show the special "problems" of interracial families. Jane Lazarre's book was the first I found in which an interracial marriage was treated as normal, in which the focus was not on race as a barrier between the woman and the man. This is not to say that Jane and

James's relationship is perfect. They do indeed argue, even scream at each other (well, Jane screams at the more controlled James). They have trouble adjusting to their new lives as parents. They struggle. However, none of these difficulties is specifically related to their racial difference but rather to differences of temperament. The social difference that causes the most trouble between them is gender, not race. James and Jane have to unlearn gender-specific behaviors and expectations in order to keep their marriage healthy. James has to learn how to be a new kind of father, a feminist co-parent, while Jane has to learn how to let him be more involved with Benjamin, to relinquish some of her mother-power.

The Mother Knot takes place in a period not long removed from the federal end of anti-miscegenation laws (with the Supreme Court's decision in Loving v. Virginia, 1967), a time when interracial marriages were unusual. The events in the book take place close to the height of Black Power rhetoric, with its excoriation of blacks who "marry white." Although Jane doesn't care what white racists think, she feels uncomfortable around some of James's black law school classmates, whom she believes tolerate her only out of respect for her husband and whom she knows disapprove of James's choice of partner. Overt and intense disapproval of interracial marriages has lessened somewhat through the succeeding years, but black-white interracial marriages remain comparatively rare (roughly 250,000 at last census) and continue to meet resistance. Given the prevalence of racism, outsiders tend to assume that people in interracial marriages have had to brave familial objections, an assumption that is often false. Jane and James enjoy the full support of their families, which Lazarre suggests in the book is an important contributing factor to their marriage's strength.

There is, however, one hugely significant absence in this circle of support and love: Jane's mother, who died when Jane was seven. After Benjamin's birth, James's mother, Marie, comes from North Carolina to help for a few weeks. Grateful as Jane is, it is not James's mother she wants but her own. Her greatest wish after giving birth is one impossible to fulfill, expressed in a variant of a child's familiar cry: "I just wanted my mother." And yet James's mother is also the mother Jane wants. "What did I care about poverty, about racism, about the small-town boredom my husband always recalled bitterly? Hadn't her children always had a mother? Hadn't she been home with them from the day of their birth until they marched victoriously off to college? Hadn't she cooked magnificent meals and baked pies for no special occasion? Hadn't all the things I had always wanted been theirs?"

If Jane cannot have Marie as her mother, then she wants to be the mother Marie was. She will be very different from her own mother, who worked outside her house, who hired help to care for her daughters, and who, of course, died and left Jane behind. Through mothering Benjamin, however, Jane recovers other parts of her experience as a daughter, drawing close again in memory to the mother she lost those many years before. On one occasion, which I take to be representative of many others, Jane is singing Benjamin to sleep when "my mother's face filled my head, pushing everything else away. And it was with her hand that I patted Benjamin's back until he was asleep and it was with her voice that I sang to him." This passage beautifully captures the profound connectedness of mothering.

And there are many such passages in The Mother Knot, passages whose resonance make me want to resurrect my teenage habit of marking exclamation points in the margins of books that seem to speak directly to me. Lazarre's book has spoken directly to many readers over the years, and I am deeply grateful to Duke University Press for giving it a chance to reach a new audience. Like only a very few books, it is a modern feminist classic, certain to leave its readers changed from the experience of reading its seldom-spoken truths.

Preface to the Duke Edition

Several years ago, I was teaching an undergraduate course called "Voices of Mothers and Daughters in Novels By Women." We had read *Jane Eyre* which introduced the great themes and classic motifs of the daughter's journey toward self-realization. And then we came to Kate Chopin's *The Awakening*, one of the first novels in English to be written by a mother who takes a mother's point of view as the subject of a literary work. When it was first published, many critics and reviewers found the heroine, Edna, to be unloving and selfish, an unnatural mother, and I had learned over years of teaching the novel that contemporary generations of students often felt the same. So before we began this story of a woman trying to chart a path to herself, struggling to become an artist, loving her children but unwilling or unable to "turn over her soul to them," I asked my students to close their eyes and think about "the good mother." As they sat there ruminating silently, I asked a few widely spaced questions: What is she like? How does she act? What do we need from her? Then I asked them to open their eyes and write down some of what had come to them. As they read out the qualities of "the good mother" I wrote them on the blackboard until it was filled with overlapping, crowded text, long sentences and single words: She is giving and caring. Unselfish. A model of independence, but she needs her children's love deeply. Highly disciplined. A disciplinarian, but she understands the need for fun. Reliable, yet childlike. Tells you right from wrong, but is never intrusive. Emotionally connected, but she can be mysterious—she has her own life! As they called out the phrases while I wrote, my students understood the pattern emerging and rolled their eyes at their own surprising beliefs. I asked them to close their eyes again. Now imagine, I said, that you are not daughters and sons but mothers. You are yourself, but you have just been told you are having a baby. The room filled with gasps and groans. Eyes snapped opened. They felt terrified, they said, of the impossible expectations. They were only human, after all. They felt inadequate. Even in an imaginary, passing moment, they already felt classic maternal guilt.

Now the silence of the moment was mine. I looked around the room at these men and women young enough to be my children, and I understood that the story of mothers from their own point of view will never be told for the last time, will never once and for all alter the deepest structures of our feelings. As long as we have children and raise them—both badly and well, as we must—the story of the mother in her own voice will have to be told and retold. We will have to break the silence and break it again as we try to become real for our children and, at the same time, come more fully to understand our society and ourselves.

Rereading the pages of this story of a new mother written over twenty years ago, I remember feeling what the writer Meena Alexander has called "the shock of arrival." Like an immigrant on foreign shores, I was stunned, uncertain of direction, trying to understand the history and culture of my new home—which was not yet anything like home to me. What strikes me most forcefully in this memoir now is the experience of pregnancy, birthing, and early motherhood as a life crisis, filled with the passion, ambivalence, and even obsession of any transformation. Now, my sons are grown, and in my work motherhood has been a primary subject, the central theme of two books which came after *The Mother Knot*. In my novel *Worlds Beyond My Control*, I wrote, in part, of how the ordinary experience of children growing up and the extraordinary experience of one of them contracting a chronic disease (in my son's case, diabetes) filled me with a sense of impotence. Yet the humility that was the hard-won, painful consequence of both ordinary and extraordinary loss deepened and sharpened my love even as it forced upon me an awareness of our separate bodies, our separate lives.

> I am forty-five years old. I have two sons, one is gone from home. The other's leaving gathers energy like a storm off the coast, and I have known hurricanes before. I begin the dreary process of battening down hatches, taping windows, packing breakables in layers of newspaper, then laying them in cartons. At night, when Anthony is out on the street, I lie in bed and practice putting old

habits away as if they were china plates I'd hoped to save forever. I cannot protect him, I tell myself in the dark. Even if at this very moment some mugger is poised for attack, even if he is lying damaged, cut and bruised, even if I imagine every possible danger and like a witch think it away, I cannot protect him. I have no control, I tell myself in the dark. There is nothing I can do now. His life. My life. Separate as sentences.

In a more recent memoir, *Beyond the Whiteness of Whiteness*, I explored the particular experience of being a white mother of Black sons, a theme already there in *The Mother Knot* but overlooked by most readers, and I tried once again to express how enmeshed these two passions of motherhood and writing have been for me:

> When I began to write seriously—that is, in a disciplined way—when I was born, in other words, into being a writer, I also had just had a child. I thought I had nothing to write about because motherhood represented only something personal, not potentially transformative or transcendent, certainly not literary. It was a revelation to read writers such as Tillie Olsen who was using her knowledge of motherhood as metaphoric, enabling her to write of many layers of human experience. I have written many different stories since that revelation, but being a mother continued to be a central passion of my life, and so it was one of the experiences I most wanted to write about, for the same reasons any writer wants to write about her passions—to name them more accurately, to understand them, to convey meaning to others, to use one's own life to think about life itself.

That theme, too, of a young writer coming into her own voice is central to *The Mother Knot*. When I wrote this memoir, I felt I belonged nowhere, certainly not to the texts and sub-texts about motherhood, whether by artists or scientists, then passing for the truth. Because of my own youth and passion, and the women's movement growing and spreading around me, my alienation and loneliness was translated into anger and the determination to write in a public voice. Since then, we have been given truer stories, not only through the recovery of old works like Kate Chopin's *The Awakening*, but by the many writers and artists who have taken up the subject of motherhood in the past two decades. From Tillie Olsen—whose classic story of maternal desperation and wisdom, "I Stand Here Ironing," was one of the seeds which began it all—through Grace Paley, Adrienne Rich, Dorothy Dinnerstein, Audre Lorde, Sara Ruddick, Alice Walker, Lynn Sharon Schwartz, Lynda Schor, Jessica Benjamin, Maureen Reddy, Sharon Olds, Lucille Clifton, Toni Morrison, Nancy Huston, Marianne Hirsch—to name only a handful in what is becoming a rich tradition—such writers and thinkers have helped me to understand our history and the meaning of my own work.

But even the most familiar, often told stories, it seems, must continually be revised. Last year, after surviving breast cancer, I found my own mother, who had died forty-five years earlier from the same disease, resurrected in my consciousness like a giantess come to claim her stolen place. From this surprising reunion came the recognition of an intriguing paradox: The "shock of arrival" had taken many years and many books for me. In novels and memoirs and in my actual life with my children, I had struggled to learn the language of a mother's voice. Now in my early fifties, forced to confront the myths I had constructed about my mother, I saw I had learned the mother's language so well I had to learn the daughter's voice again.

When I reread The Mother Knot today, I hear that voice, the young woman trying to learn how to be a mother while she is longing for a mother herself. She can be righteous, of course, full of fierce conviction, but she shouts the recognition of desire and the need for love.

And yet, her language is indeed my mother-tongue, because if it was as my sons' mother that I first garnered the courage to write my stories for the world, it was as my mother's daughter that I looked squarely at the terror of belonging nowhere and began to recover some of the places where I belong. The mother knot tightens and loosens for me. Protecting and constraining, it is the source of my own awakening.

Jane Lazarre

January 1997

Acknowledgments

As I anticipate this edition of *The Mother Knot*, by Duke University Press, I would like to express special thanks to those who enabled me to write this memoir so many years ago, and to those who have supported it since.

Many friends, old and new, and too numerous to mention here, have helped to clarify my thinking and feeling about the experience of motherhood that is central to this book and to my life. Again, I express my appreciation to them all.

Joyce Johnson edited the original manuscript and was primarily responsible for bringing the work into the world.

In the most recent past, the life of this book has been sustained by several people whose help and encouragement I would like to acknowledge here: my agent, Wendy Weil, whose integrity and friendship I value in so many ways; Sara Ruddick, whose support for my work has been invaluable to me as a friend and as a writer; Maureen Reddy, whose writing about my work has often sustained me; Tillie Olsen, whose own work is both standard and inspiration to anyone concerned with either motherhood or the poetry of language; and Nancy Huston, whose work has revealed so exquisitely the experience of both motherhood and daughterhood.

I am deeply grateful to all the people at Duke University Press for their support of my work. I especially thank my editor, Valerie Millholland, and everyone in the marketing department, with very special appreciation for Emily Young.

The words I wrote for the first edition about my sister, Emily Lazarre, still stand: it is through my lifelong love for her that I come to understand ever more profoundly the experiences of motherhood, daughterhood, and sisterhood.

My mother-in-law, Lois Meadows White, helped me in many ways during the writing of this book and has continued her support in many ways since.

As always in my work, I thank my family—Douglas Hughes White, Adam Lazarre-White, and Khary Lazarre-White—for all they have taught me, for their understanding, and for their friendship.

Preface

It is rare to read, whether in literature or social science, about the experience of motherhood as described by mothers themselves. On the contrary, most of what we read about motherhood are descriptions of mothers from the points of view of the children—grown-up children who are now psychologists, anthropologists or writers, but, existentially and in relation to the people they are describing, children nevertheless. Thus, as is so often the case in scientific knowledge, unconscious desires and needs are hopelessly entwined with what might seem to be purely analytical statement. When women professionals, who may also be mothers, have sought to contribute to our knowledge of this complicated experience, in the field of psychoanalysis, for example, they have to a large degree been overly influenced by the ubiquitous Western myth of placid, fulfilling maternity which has been accepted by their male teachers and mentors, and they, therefore, like their male counterparts, have given us only half the story. And the vicious circle is complete; the myth determines the content of our so-called "objective knowledge" and our knowledge is used to reinforce the myth. And the myth, which holds such sway over all the mothers I know, is destructive precisely because it is not altogether wrong, but leaves out half of the truth.

Although women are as different from one another as men are, although we have developed into many different kinds of personalities through endlessly varied experiences, although we are born with every kind of human temperament—still there is only one image in this culture of the "good mother." At her worst, this mother image is a tyrannical goddess of stupefying love and murderous masochism whom none of us can or should hope to emulate. But even at her best, she is only one limited sort of person, not the vast treasure house of human possibility which would be the stuff of a creative and nourishing cultural myth. She is quietly strong, selflessly giving, undemanding, unambitious; she is receptive and intelligent in only a moderate, concrete way; she is of even temperament, almost always in control of her emotions. She loves her children completely and unambivalently.

Most of us are not like her. Try as we might, in our most self-doubting, isolated hours with our children, our real selves come back again and again to haunt us. Yet we want children. And we love our children as immeasurably and intensely as that "good mother," if she exists at all. Since our experience is not described, we have to begin from the beginning—to speak about what it is really like. Only in this way can we hope to change the conclusions and theories which always hover on the edge of our experience, demanding that we sacrifice our self-knowledge to their established vision of the truth.

Both feminist women and men who have assumed complete care of their young children have written extensively in the past few years about the terrible details which engulf a mother's life, about the strange and paradoxical way in which the infinite kind of love we feel for our children is locked into the dull, enervating routine of caring for them, especially when our entire lives are devoted to that responsibility. But it is particularly difficult for women to break out of this pattern.

Rather, it is seductively easy to give up everything for our children—those beings who once shared our very bodies. For the separation is never total. Every year, before my son's birthday, I feel mild labor pains and the tingling of milk moving in my breasts. This dimension of our relationship is extremely difficult to overcome and it often threatens to edge us beyond the normal limits of identification.

But, it seems to me, much of what has been called "neurotic" in the woman and "pathogenic" for the child in psychological literature is, on the contrary, a normal part of the experience of being a mother, probably for always, but certainly in the first few years and especially with the first child. The only thing which seems to me to be eternal and natural in motherhood is ambivalence and its manifestation in the ever ongoing cycles of separation and unification with our children.

This is the story of the first period of crisis in motherhood experienced by one woman. She is of course an individual and in that sense she is atypical: she is an artist; she is temperamentally intense and she is middle class in a certain cultural sense although she has no money for housekeepers, full-time baby-sitters and secluded, private offices. But she is also completely typical in that she is a human being who is a woman and a mother, and it is in that sense that her experiences might reflect those of other women, might even help to demolish that impossible set of standards which oppresses us all—the motherhood mystique.

Part One
Birth

This eye

is not for weeping

its vision

must be unblurred

though tears are on my face

its intent is clarity

it must forget

nothing

ADRIENNE RICH

from "From the Prison House"

9/71

I

was terrified. Had been for two months. During my first labor, four years before, I had been innocent, allaying my fears with the knowledge that birth is a natural process. This time I was wiser. Euphemisms, whether medical or mystical, no longer held any weight with me. My only hope was that, instead of the twenty-four-hour labor I had suffered with my first child, this one would be short.

The nurse wouldn't let James come in with me and the minute he left me my fear increased. The pains were still mild, a real contraction coming only every twenty minutes or so. But in between, anxiety would cramp my stomach, convincing me I was two minutes away from the delivery table. "Relax and it will hurt less," people had told me, suggesting that there was really nothing to be frightened of, as if the source of the pain were my imagination instead of my uterus. But I had determined that it was best to face this night with an uncompromising realism. So until my husband walked through the door again, I paced and wept, not yet in pain, only in fear.

At the beginning of our love affair, seven years before, he had told me how he hated conflict. Coming from a loud-talking, deep-feeling family, most of whom were constantly involved in trying to figure themselves and each other out, he had been the one to withdraw from childhood on. He would run up to his room to escape the suffocating flow of human feeling. Or he would go to the field behind his house and lie down in the grass to clear his head and think of nothing but the reed he chewed in his teeth. Intensity was a burden. If he ever expressed his own, he did it on the football field or in early, passionate sex, but not in talk, not even in remembered dreams. It was as if there had been some agreement made at an uncertain moment in the past, an agreement which designated James as the child who would express the silent controls lacked by everyone else, who would run in a straight line toward the goal while everyone else spilled all over the field.

The family would be listening to the radio, the television and the record player simultaneously in three different rooms, an animated discussion would be taking place in the kitchen, and they all would wait for James's predictable plea for something, anything, to be turned off. While everyone else in the large family found solace and strength in sharing all the details, each and every nuance, of the problems of their individual lives, James developed the need for strict privacy; he kept his business to himself, he would say. And he would inevitably decide to read a magazine during the frequent emotional confrontations.

James loved his family; so much so that when he married he chose someone much more like them than like himself. Perhaps he needed the familiar, open, relentlessly shared feeling to keep him in touch with his own boundaries. Maybe he had grown comfortable playing the quiet role to someone else's intensity. In any case, he did not marry a controlled sort of woman who could be counted on to keep her deepest feelings tucked neatly out of sight; he married me.

Finally the nurse allowed him into the dingy room, paint peeling from the walls, the air conditioner making the sound of several hundred horses galloping down a road full of sloshing water. Just the right atmosphere for concentrated breathing, panting and blowing. I was only up to the first stage of the breathing and already I was losing control. The Lamaze Method. I had sworn never to believe their insidious promises again. James grinned at me when he saw me sitting down seriously on the hospital bed, trying to pant in rhythm to "Mary Had a Little Lamb." I grinned, too, and said, Shit. That had been our attitude throughout the last six weeks. When we could bring ourselves to practice, alone and with our friends who were also expecting their second child, we always ended up laughing after ten minutes and abandoned the effort. We had learned with our first child, we thought, that the entire sect of natural childbirth was a big fat defense mechanism against pain. In one Pacific Island culture, the women beat themselves with sharp sticks during labor, perhaps a more diverting physical exercise than breathing like a dog in heat. But in both cases, the assumption is the same: the more you can manage to think of something else, the more you will be able to endure the horror going on in your uterus.

But I am not the type to endure. Falling short of the revolutionary image passed on to me through my father's dreams, I can only in fantasy withstand the fascist torture while refusing to divulge the names of my comrades. In truth, I am afraid that the moment they even threaten to hurt me, I will tell all.

Movies, so popular in my generation, which depict people suffering all sorts of physical pain upset me for days, creep into my nights and make my insomnia worse. Not that I want to be this way. I want to be brave—an amazon. And when it comes to tolerating mental pain, I am definitely in the race. But my body is weak. Just its ability to go on living is a miracle to me.

When James grinned, I lost the grasp I had on the tail end of the Lamaze illusion. "Might just as well wait for the pain," I said. "Chances are I will still be alive by morning." Remembering the short, fifteen minutes of transition (that terror-filled time of labor when you feel a steel rod pushing apart your insides) which I had experienced with my first child, I felt I could take it.

So for the next three hours I simply lay there and suffered, a little more with each contraction, and pretended to breathe correctly so I wouldn't have an argument with the obstetrician. At least I wasn't spitting forth green vomit into James's arms like the last time. I submitted to the shaving of my perineum, nearly coming in the nurse's palm, tried to drive away the fears of pain and death, and concentrated on my son and my sister whose dependency on me always succeeded in increasing my evident strength and self-restraint. I was convinced I would deliver by 5 A.M. One nurse even bet her tuna-fish sandwich on it. And that it would be a typical second birth—tolerable if not easy.

Therefore, I was totally unprepared for the two hours and fifty-nine minutes of transition during which I screamed continually, begging for them to cut me open or end my life. I must have squeezed the blood out of James's hand as the nurses held my legs apart while I tried to push the baby's head into position. They gave me Pitocin to speed up contractions which, my feminist sisters had warned me, made the pains more intense and less controllable. But who cared. At least they would be over faster. I wanted it to be over. I wanted to be alive. I wanted James to get home to our little boy, Benjamin, who, I was convinced, was suffering a trauma of separation. Then I let them give me Demerol, knowing that any last hope of controlling the contractions would be gone as I drifted in and out of foggy and nauseous slumber, wakened only by the pain in my anus—("Very common to feel the pressure in your anus with the second child, young lady")—or shrieks coming from very far away. In the two or three minutes of consciousness during the contraction I would know those shrieks were my own, but they were eerily beyond my control.

"Don't scream," the gentle nurse warned me, "or you'll take energy away from the pushing." And, Lord knows, I wanted to stop that ridiculous yelling, only I couldn't. My mouth would open as if by itself and the screaming would start.

I hadn't heard that kind of screaming since I had gone crazy as a child and heard my mother, dead from cancer, screaming in my head, breaking my eardrums from the inside.

I could no longer see clearly but I felt James's arm. I wanted him to think me strong, grown up. Like him. Not like my tired, confused self, my inner strength almost broken from the pressures of maternity.

On the delivery table, I had lost the faith that I would live. I was afraid to touch my vagina or my anus—knowing that my hand would return dripping with my own precious blood. "Hemorrhaged on the delivery table," I could hear the doctor say as he emerged from the room. Iron clamps covered most of my forearms. Green leggings hung from my thighs. A white hospital gown covered my breasts and some horrible leather mask was pushing down on my face. Only my vagina was uncovered.

Do you love me now, Jamie?

"Push," the doctor said, and I thought he meant to kill me. My asshole was splitting open, pouring forth blood, I thought, drenching the hospital floor. Down the hall I heard another woman scream and drift off into constant anguish-filled moans.

"Close the door, we can't listen to that," said my doctor.

"Push," James said. So I obeyed, thinking, Good-by, my darling, you don't realize that I'm dying but I am and I will never again return to you, the dark well of pain is opening up for me and this last time I will not find my way out take care of Benjamin my darling boy and know that I want to die now, I don't mind, except for leaving you

at which point my second son was born.

It was pointless to wonder, lying in the recovery room drifting in and out of sleep—last vestige of the various chemicals which had finally helped me reach the delivery table—why I had dared come to this once more after swearing in another hospital four years before that I would never do it again. All I could remember was that at some moment, fully aware of how difficult I found motherhood to be, I had desperately wanted another child. I wanted to be pregnant again, I wanted to give birth again, I even wanted another newborn baby.

When I was fully awake, I asked for my baby. When they brought him to me, his dark eyes opened and his mouth started searching for a wet nipple. I could see his pointy chin, so much like my first baby's in the early weeks of life. The smell of blood and sweat faded as the aroma of a brand-new baby surrounded me. I shed tears all over his little face as I remembered the pain only several hours behind me, and I knew that, incredibly, I would still love him.

After three days, I went home to my apartment. For an hour I rested in the cleanliness and order James had created for my homecoming, and in the silence bestowed by the absence of Benjamin, who was still at his day-care center.

Whether or not this one is a "good baby," I told myself, I am a different person, more comfortable as a mother, knowing that soon he too will leave the house each day with his lunch box under his arm and refuse to let me kiss him whenever I want to.

When my own private form of what the experts call "post-partum depression" began to take hold of me, I noted that it was exactly the same as the last time: I wanted only to lie still and quiet in a semidark and perfectly, but absolutely, clean room. I wanted someone else to do everything except feed the baby. When not feeding, I wanted James all to myself. And I dreaded the sound of a human voice.

Still, in spite of this exact repetition of my first experience, I believed that I was a different person. This time it would be different.

When Benjamin came home from the day-care center, I wanted to hold him so badly that my hands sweated waiting for him to come up in the elevator. As he came toward me I saw myself, twenty-seven years before, when they brought my sister home and I looked up at my mother and father, omniscient giants that they were, not quite knowing how my life would change but feeling certain that it would never be the same again.

Passing me by, tiptoeing around the woman who had become in a frightening moment the mother of someone else, he walked right over to the carriage to peer at his brother. For the next few weeks he would hate me often for bringing him this thing he had repeatedly asked for, the brother I had grown in my belly for nine exhausting months so that my lovely boy could have a sibling. And once he got over the initial phase of anger there would be something different in his eyes.

In those early days, all the mythical aspects of motherhood hung in the air around us. And once again I tried to piece all of our expectations into the image of a beautiful woman whose being I would then don like a golden gown. I took Benjamin's fantasies, James's embellished childhood memories and my own, the baby's satisfied face when he drank from my breast and the paintings of a thousand ethereal mothers and tried to weave them into the pattern of a strong but gentle amazon whose body I might gracefully inhabit.

Mother, goddess of love, to whom we all can go for protection and unconditional love, perfect human being we have all been taught to believe in, whom poets have compared to the earth itself, who kneels down, arms outstretched, to enclose us and fend off the rains, whom none of us has ever met but who continues to haunt us mercilessly; Mother, I can't find you, let alone be you.

For that heroine whom I expected to rise out of my bed each morning, looking like plain old me but surrounded by the magic of maternity, did not appear. No matter what any of us thought or cherished, consciously or unconsciously, secretly or out loud, I was not that person. I just wanted my mother.

2

My mother had died when I was seven. For many years I lived primarily to search for her. I would pretend to find her in every new woman I met. I imagined her to be hiding behind walls, on the other side of mirrors, within my favorite photographs of her. But I never quite convinced myself that she had returned to me. For a while I tried secretly being her. But that only made the confusion worse. I ended up, during my teen-age years, holding on to reality by my fingernails, unsure whether I wanted to be her, the price of which was the loss of myself, or to be myself without her.

By the time I reached my early twenties, I had chosen to be myself. I no longer thought about her every moment of my life. I took her picture out of the secret compartment of my wallet.

For about five years I was free. Then I got pregnant and she returned to me, but in a new way. When my first baby was still a tadpole inside me, she came into my dreams. She came as a wise priestess offering love and encouragement. She came as herself, but with a vividness I had not experienced in my conscious life for eighteen years. Her face would be there, looking at me in the darkness, just the way it had been when I had known her. I saw aspects of her features that I had forgotten so long ago, articles of her clothing, the texture of her hair. One night she came as a witch. She seemed to be warning me. She seemed to know something I didn't.

I woke up from my dream and moved my expanding body close to James, flattening my stomach against his back. I knew that I would sleep away the morning. I hoped I wouldn't stare away the afternoon, pretending I had no work to do, rushing for a mystery to read, a movie on television, or a hot-fudge sundae.

I had gone for the pregnancy test as a lark. My friend Carla knew the lab technician at Yale New Haven Hospital so, never having had a pregnancy test before, I decided to try it. I felt certain, however, that my period was two months late only because I had recently stopped taking the pill and gone back to the diaphragm, greasy friend of my teen-age years which did not present the danger of an early death. The doctor had said late periods were common in such cases.

It had never occurred to me to have a child. James had been accepted by this prestigious university, poor boy from North Carolina making unbelievably good. I was anxious to leave New York for a while, and I had great plans for the years ahead of me.

Behind me were five years of full-time jobs in a hectic city. After college, I had spent a year working for the Welfare Department learning the futility of everything I tried to do, crushing any illusions about the romance of poverty. I learned about my complete impotence in the face of the enormous human misery I encountered every day; I grew more and more frightened of the streets lined with jeering, gaping men yelling epithets or sneering sexual invitations. I began to go home on my field days when I was supposed to be visiting clients. Then I would write in my diary—or record books, as I had begun to call them. I wrote in my record books to keep track of my life, I would say. But there was more to it than that.

I had always been periodically confused by the intensity of my feelings. They came, at times, ferociously, each new emotion contradicting in a split second the one which had come before. When I tried to sort it all out quietly, wordlessly, I would find myself sinking in a quicksand of unclear thoughts, my eyes burning, my body sweating, my head aching. Only through writing it all out in my record book did I learn to achieve a sort of calm.

While I was writing, the thoughts kept coming, getting all tangled, unrecognizable, oppressive. I could not grasp them for long enough to hear them. But if I continued to write, a process began, a sort of a translation of the tension into words; and the words created the possibility for clarity to develop. Just keep writing, I had learned. Soon punctuation would appear, sentences became shorter. Things would clear away. And suddenly I would focus on the central point which had been hidden, smothered by the rest. When the central point was visible at last, I was relieved for a moment. I would feel as though I had organized a huge pile of debris, cleaned out an overstuffed closet. Only later, hours perhaps or even days, would I realize that the debris was what had been precious all along. The main point, the thing I had been calling "central," was something I had always known, what I could have said in the first place had I simply been in a different mood. But it was insufficient, insubstantial, ridiculous all by itself. It was and is always the debris which is the treasure, for the debris is all that connects that final point to everything else in my life.

For me, living without writing things down has always been confusing. I never feel as if I understand anything until it is described over and over at great length. Months or years later, after the time which has given me such great sadness or happiness or fear or pleasure is past, I sit down by myself and read over what I have written. Then I think, Oh, so that's what happened. I see now how I felt.

When I started working for the Welfare Department, I began a new book whose entries were kept religiously, neatly, holders, as they were, of all the discipline which the rest of my life lacked. I wrote about my "cases," the women I met whose children stared at me, it seemed, from every doorway. I wrote about old Mr. Fields, with whom I spent one day a week talking about his daughter in foster care, his alcoholic wife, his crippled leg. I wrote about the children in foster care, describing their faces, exorcising them for one relief-filled minute, until inevitably the pain returned and I could no longer separate their sense of abandonment from my own.

Soon my neglect of my clients, however irrelevant it was to their lives, began to keep me awake nights, and I quit the job. For the next year, I worked in a quiet library doing undemanding work; I typed labels, filed cards, shelved books, saved my energy for the evenings, when I took out my record book to write of my dreams, my childhood, rhetorical demands for political justice, detailed descriptions of passionate sexual experiences or miserable accounts of my shame.

When boredom began to grow out of my uneventful days I took a job teaching English at a neighborhood high school. Despite my initial terror of the infamous teen-agers waiting for me in rowdy classrooms, I was elated by the prospect of returning to the "real" world. I was able to learn over a period of years how to talk to the students, even how to teach them. All of my energy was spent thinking about those one hundred and sixty faces, only several years younger than my own, which stared out at me expectantly every day. On certain days I returned home greatly excited. Perhaps a student had written a composition about how her English teacher had revealed to her the beauties of poetry; or a boy had spoken to me at length about his difficulties with love, so like my own. On other days, the despair was blinding. A class had mocked me for my tiring lesson or my white skin. A girl who wrote beautiful poetry had sat nodding throughout the class, showing the unmistakable signs of her first experience with drugs. A boy I felt had great intelligence had been exposed as the richest pusher in the junior class. This world, totally new to me and more complex than I had ever imagined, drew me completely. I had time for nothing else. I wrote in my record books only on weekends and vacations; I had an idea for my first novel, but I had time only for developing an outline.

During this period I married James, and shortly afterward he was accepted to law school. I decided to stop teaching and to accompany him to New Haven, not only because I wanted to be with him; I was also eager to write my book. I found a boring undemanding job again, this time as a secretary, and saved my real energy for writing. I struggled to finish my clerical tasks in half the time allotted and spent the rest of my day writing on the classy I.B.M. electric.

In one way and another, in my record books, in my dreams, in my experiences, I had been writing this book for five years. Now it was just a question of putting the words on paper, and by the middle of the year I had a first draft. But for the rewriting, I needed advice from older writers I knew, I needed my friends in the evenings. I needed more money. None of which was available to me in New Haven. The only people I knew were James's classmates. Even James was so busy at night from the demands of the first semester of law school, that he barely had time to say hello. So I decided to move back to New York. James and I agreed that seeing each other on weekends, when I would come to New Haven, made more sense as a living arrangement for the time being. And though I would miss him, I anticipated moving back to New York with great excitement.

Then I missed my period for the second month in a row and casually made an appointment for the test I knew would be negative.

If I am really pregnant, I thought as I handed the Tropicana orange juice bottle filled with my urine to the lab technician, what a lovely place to have this wonderful experience, to fulfill both sides of my nature, having a baby while I write my book. For I already knew that if by some chance I were going to have a baby, I would not move away from James.

The woman in the white lab coat looked at me with shocked eyes as I handed her the huge bottle. But I was not embarrassed until I saw Carla, also waiting anxiously for a late period, hand her a very genteel pill bottle with several drops of pee inside.

"Really wanted to be sure, didn't you?" smirked the young woman who was going to perform the test. But I had never been at this juncture in life before. I imagined they needed a lot of urine to inject into the rabbit I expected her to produce.

Instead she dropped a tiny piece of litmus paper into each bottle.

"If the test is negative, it may be wrong," she said smartly, "but if it's positive, it's definitely valid."

To my nervous friend, on the verge of a separation from her husband, she pronounced the relieving word, "Negative."

Then she turned back to the flasks and dropped paper into mine. A minute later she looked at me over her shoulder. "You're pregnant," she said.

I looked back at her, feeling as if she had told me I was actually a Martian and had only been adopted by an Earth family in infancy.

"Fuck," I said, my eyes wide with wonder.

The lab technician stared me down for a long moment. "You ought to be thankful," she said.

And, in truth, I was not unhappy. In retrospect, I am sure that for months I had been trying to get pregnant without quite knowing it. I had misused the diaphragm—I who had always counted the eight hours to the minute before removing the rubber disc from the hook of my uterus; who had buried it in so much jelly that I would drip gooey blobs all the way back to the bed; who held it up to the light faithfully every time, as the doctor had taught me when I was sixteen, to spot the insidious pinhole which would betray me; who, as my friends had abortion after abortion, had never made that frightening trip to Puerto Rico or Canada; who was innocent of the dirty tables and the dangers of hemorrhaging and the five hundred dollars blown in an afternoon. This time I had knowingly used a diaphragm which fit badly. I had left it in for days at a time. I had never held it up to the light.

After all, I was married to a man I loved. I knew I wanted children someday, so why not now? I was already imagining my baby, strapped to my back, as I typed my book, went to fancy restaurants, climbed mountains; my son or daughter would sleep while I worked, and every four hours or so I would stop to nurse from my breast, the breast my mother, a successful business woman, had never had the leisure to offer me. I wouldn't need the maids she had relied upon to bring me up. I would take care of my own child and continue to live my own life too.

So it was not that I was disappointed when my urine registered positive. It was that no one I knew had a child, except my father and my aunts and uncles and their friends. Only grownups were parents and I was still a child. In that instant, my sense of who I was flipped over. I almost fell down as I walked back toward the elevator and it was not from the hormones which had suddenly and magically gone into attack.

I imagined James—proud and joyful. I imagined my father's happy voice and James's parents who had begun talking about their grand-children on our wedding day. Then, in the moment of thinking about my baby's grandparents, I began to sense the complicated world which awaited my child. My father would be waiting for the Jewish intel-lectual his grandchild would surely be, the inheritor of generations of Old World culture and New World socialism, a member of the army fighting for social justice, a servant to the people, a traveler in the grandfather's footsteps. Meanwhile, my father-in-law would be expect-ing a Black warrior, surpassing James in athletic agility and academic achievement. He would know how to control his life in a world which was demanding and unjust. In an ocean of failures, he would succeed. And he would be rich.

James and I were not, I realized once again, just any old couple holding hands in Central Park, making up from a fight before drifting off to sleep, failing each other at times and fulfilling each other as best we could. We were a political entity: Black man married to white woman.

It had been one thing to understand racism and to hate it as I saw it affecting people I had come to love. It was quite another to imagine my own child having to struggle against the world in ways I had not experienced until I was past twenty. Love for my baby filled me, along with a new anger at a world in which I had felt myself to be a stranger, in which I lived only as a result of the greatest exertion. Having felt slightly apart all of my life, it was not any quest for social acceptance which my baby's racial identity threatened. In fact, I had always felt self-righteous about the struggles of other white people married to Blacks. If they had difficulties in adjusting to niggerhood in the white world, I didn't pity them. It was a purification ceremony that could do nothing but help their characters. If they had married Blacks for the neurotic reasons described by Cleaver, that was their psychic funeral. I dismissed white racists without a trace of ambivalence, having learned as the child of Jewish Communists that I was not now nor ever had been a member of the American club. Black rejection was more difficult to deal with. Perhaps Blacks had a right to be racists. Though I had never felt the remotest connection to southern whites of the eighteenth century, maybe I was, in some existential sense, the descendant of slaveholders.

As Carla and I walked back toward the law school, I almost felt the baby grow inside me, and I suddenly felt completely Black. My friend, who was Black, scoffed at my naïveté, and certainly her cultural past and the special awareness it gave her were not suddenly my own. James and I were just as different, sprung from entirely different traditions. But in that moment, walking down the street full of people who were miraculously unaware of the change in me, resting my hand lightly on my belly, I was as Black as anyone.

Then I began to wonder how the Black law students would react to me when they heard of the Black child growing inside me. They had tolerated me politely out of respect for James. But the Black woman who was living with a white man did not enjoy the same generous treatment. In either case, it was the woman who was considered blameworthy. Would this new development cause them to openly reject a Black man who was so obviously "sleeping white"? How would James himself react to the possibility of a child who might look entirely white?

Walking into the darkened halls of the old law school, I felt the first sting of the loss of my selfhood, a feeling which would grow to enormous proportions in the next four years. But at that first moment, I thought it was just the weight of the secret I carried inside. James saw me from down the hall and knew immediately what had happened. But another Black student, Carla's husband, approached us first, anxious that his life should continue without this interruption. He had always made my unfortunate skin color the primary block to our relationship. He could not understand why James, a proud Black man, strong and soulful, had married a "Jewish hippie" instead of a Black queen. He never looked closely enough to see how James and I fitted each other— how in so many indescribable ways we were alike. In fact, racism being what it is, only a few people could see in us what we saw in ourselves.

Often, James and I would joke about ourselves as an "interracial couple." We would sit in the living room, comfortable in each other's presence as are any two people who have lived together for years. Suddenly, I would look at his little black curls, his broad nose, his brown skin, and say—Hey, you're a Neee-gro. Or he would look at my straighter hair, fairer skin, thinner nose and say in mock surprise—Hey woman, you white? It's true. When you are close to people you forget. It seemed to me that James had kinky hair because that was how his hair was, not because he was Black.

But when I saw Ronald approach me in the law school, my face flushed hot with my fears of his open rejection, and I knew exactly what color I was. What if he walked right by? What if he said something awful? What if he spat at me? When he came close to us, his wife announced, "She's pregnant." And when he hesitated, she ordered, "Kiss her." Embarrassed and confused, he planted that perfunctory kiss on my white cheek. I thought he would gag.

I prayed I would not feel the same discomfort envelop me when James's parents, brothers and sister kissed me. Or when my own father discovered he was to be the grandfather of a brown baby. Both of our families had supported us, loved us, told us it didn't matter. But now IT was going to be a concrete person.

James walked down the hall to me and held me. Neither of us knew what to say or really what was happening. My plans to move to New York were over. But I was not worried in those first hours of the change in my life. I would still rewrite my book, I thought quickly, not waiting for any dubious inner voice to be heard. I would quit my job, we would live off scholarships and loans, so I would be able to concentrate on writing and still have time for resting, walking, exercising, doing all the things which I vaguely knew pregnancy demanded. I pushed my face into the folds of James's big, tan coat, hiding my head in his arms. We were both smiling.

It was odd not to have to worry about birth control. It should have freed me, I told myself, to a sexual abandon hitherto unexperienced in my life. But, unfortunately, floor-to-ceiling mirrors faced our bed; whoever designed those mirrored closet doors had a more supple body than mine in mind.

All of my life I had struggled to see my body as being beautiful even though my big breasts always seemed so ungainly when compared to the subtle, boyish chests ornamenting the *New York Times Magazine* every Sunday. I could never shop in cute little boutiques. All of their cute little dresses were made with cute little bosoms in mind. Shopping for a bathing suit had always been a miserable experience because most suits were made with size A or B cups, and the salesladies would emphatically deny that anyone so young could wear more than a B.

I hadn't worn a B since I was twelve. But it seemed that not only were big breasts banished from the lovely pages of designers' notebooks and magazines, they were also erased from the consciousness of the masses.

Still, valiantly I had worked to love myself, concentrating with all my might on Sophia Loren each time Audrey Hepburn danced gracefully behind my eyes. Now, however, when I looked into that mirror at the foot of our bed and saw my naked body next to James, my vaginal canal suddenly felt as dry as an old sponge forgotten under the sink for months. I couldn't believe the sight of myself, belly protruding and breasts huger than they had ever been with nipples which had suddenly doubled their size. No one had ever told me to expect such things. I was outraged.

But being as well schooled as anyone in sexual duplicity, I was determined not to let James know that the last thing on my mind was his gentle hand or his erect penis. I tried to pretend that upsetting glance had not occurred and made heavy noises of passion. Of course I had been party to such fantasy before, so I played the part well, grunting and breathing for his pleasure, until I farted. And he laughed. That laugh, which might once have been a comfortable sign of our closeness, was now humiliating, infuriating, the final confirmation of the disgustingness of myself. I pulled away from him and began one of those uncontrollable crying fits experienced by pregnant women. You begin crying about one small, or at least concrete, incident and end up weeping about everything in your life, past and present, known and unknown, personal and cosmic. The man sits and looks at you in alarm as the hours pass by and you are still crying. And eventually he tells you that it is obviously your pregnancy which is causing this extreme reaction, implying that your sadness or anger is somehow not valid in itself. Which is exactly what James said after an hour of my weeping had drenched his chest, the sweat of sex long dried up and replaced by my tears. And that implication turned my sadness to fury in a flash.

It was months before I could make love gaily, enjoyably again. And even then, unable to experience my body as desirable in the flesh, I imagined myself (eyes tightly closed against reality) looking the way I had always dreamed I could look if only I managed to diet for long enough. My breasts would be diminished by the fifty situps I would do every day for years; my stomach would be flattened by the miles of road I would bicycle, my cheeks sunk in magnificent emaciation.

James insisted that he found me attractive and could not understand why I couldn't see myself the same way. Then I would become sarcastic, refusing to believe him. I thought he knew exactly how I must feel but was trying to convince me of an obvious fantasy just to be nice. It wasn't until five years later, when hundreds of days of motherhood had convinced me of the many differences between mothers and fathers, that I finally accepted the fact that neither James nor any other man would ever understand pregnancy. It was an obvious truth which our grandmothers had known from the start.

"There are many things men don't understand," they had said softly to us in the kitchen, far away from our fathers' ears.

But we, the reborn feminists of the late sixties, still wanted to deny it. After all, we were seeking to share everything.

So when I withdrew from sexual desire and wanted only my own side of the bed in the dark, I left James just as confused and unprepared as I was. No one had ever warned us. I thought I was becoming frigid. I was sure he would seek out another woman in whom he could express his frustrated passion. He would probably choose a Black queen.

During the next few months, unaware that there was still a world left outside of my belly, I was unable to begin the rewriting of my novel. That task demanded discipline and attention, two abilities which were more and more retreating into the realms of memory. I only wrote chaotically in my record books. For weeks sentences exploded out of me tearing through my head like a geyser ripping the earth behind it. But I was never able to achieve the decency of a long, connected paragraph. Even pronouns eluded me.

Feels very much as if I am losing my mind.

Spent five days just sitting in the house reading. Can't look at another printed page.

No meaning to anything I do. Neurosis returns in full force.

New Haven is a toilet bowl with the flusher broken. Nothing to do here. No one to talk to.

I am tempted to spend the rest of my life staring into space. Tension and anxiety very high. Must be awful for the baby.

Fantasy world is expanding. Eating up the rest of my life. Dreamt about a T.V. actor on Mission Impossible. He was making love to me. Then I had a masturbation fantasy about him during the day. Couldn't stop thinking about him. A man I don't know. A person whom I've only seen in black and white.

It must be more than New Haven. This isolation. Why do I feel so lonely? What started this cycle of depression? I understand nothing. I just stare.

Then one day, I wrote:

There has been a renaissance of joy. I feel my baby move inside. I think it will be Benjamin or Rachel. This is the most wonderful thing I've ever done.

Once before, as a child, I had been unsure of everything I felt. But then it was because my feelings were far too treacherous and shocking to admit, so I retreated out of my head down into my gut where I lived in fear of my hatreds and my loves.

Now I was always uncertain again. But instead of being caught in a tangle of too many thoughts, I was swinging back and forth between my ever present contradictions. First I was jerked in one direction, bumping hard into my revulsion at the sight of my body, knowing that I should have had an abortion, feeling an unhappiness which I was sure must indicate my unfitness as a future mother. Then I would swing back, holding on to consciousness for dear life, frightened of retreating into fantasy or dream.

Not knowing who I was, mother or child, I clung frantically to the details which proved my unified reality. I collected baby clothes. I painted cribs and highchairs. I spoke about pregnancy to anyone who would listen. Usually exquisitely responsive to the feelings of others, always courting acceptance, now I didn't care if my listeners yawned behind their hands as I droned on about my nausea, my sleepless nights, my popped-out bellybutton. I kept right on talking, encouraged by the voice which was insisting that I was someone familiar, as I swung back into the secure and comfortable pillows of love for my baby.

Tears came easily. Loving my big belly as it moved around, rippling before my astonished eyes, I stroked it gently, certain that my baby could feel my touch and at least have that experience to add to the swirling acid of my anxiety. I wept for joy, and I squeezed my nipples so that the milk would come out strong when it was needed. Incredibly, there was someone I had not yet met whom I would love as much as I did my sister, my father, James.

We came to New York for the summer—my seventh and eighth months—and stayed with my father. There was something joyful, fine and tantalizing about living in my old home. And yet, when I sat in the big chair where my mother had waited for me to be born, my father would look at me and cry. He would say things about remembering me as a baby and a little girl and talk about how much I reminded him of my mother. I found him tiring, I thought. Really, his identification of me with my mother scared me. I turned my face away from him and insisted that I was only myself. And almost losing myself in the cycles of time, I stopped sitting in the big blue chair.

Now I understand that my father was watching his own life through a window—seeing all the days and nights of his youth in my face and my belly. If I had been wiser then, I might have been kinder and sat longer in the blue chair, allowing him to look. But I wasn't a mother yet and so my father was still only my father to me. Not until I had lived that long and painful ceremony of parenthood which slowly molded me into some kind of grownup did I understand that my father was only a man, who among other experiences, had raised two children.

Once, several years later, I must have been looking at Benjamin in the same way. He looked back at me, uncomfortable and annoyed, and said, "Mommy, would you stop looking at me like that!" Thirty years of memories were too heavy for him to bear. And he turned around to the string he was using to tie all the furniture together, just as I had walked away from the big blue chair and my father's eyes.

One of the pleasures of that summer in New York was that I had started graduate school in anthropology. For five months I had been unable to work on my novel, and my growing fears of being nothing but pregnant had driven me to make a new choice. Now that I was involved in my classes, forced to concentrate on something other than my own body, it seemed to me that I had done the right thing. It was not important at the time that I knew I was settling for something I had never really wanted. I had something to do. I felt alive, as if I belonged on the city streets as much as anyone. I was not just wandering, I was going somewhere. It didn't matter if I dawdled or stopped to look in the shops. I was secure. People could see that I was busy. Images of pregnant women relinquishing all their passions, stacking their dreams on a useless shelf to be picked up when the children were grown, were banished from my mind.

Besides, hadn't everyone always expected me to be a scholar? My father, the professor in school to whom I was most drawn—hadn't they all rewarded me with compliments about my intelligence in the form of A's and kisses?

"My girl," my father had said as I received A after A in my courses.

"Great potential," my professor had said, smiling.

Even James seemed to love me more, proudly announcing to friends and family that I would someday be addressed "Doctor." What better way to hoard such security than by continuing to do what I knew how to do well—take tests and write papers? Certainly the material was interesting. So I banished the knowledge that with all these classes to attend and textbooks to read I had no time to work on my novel. I kept track of my pregnancy in my record book. And no longer threatened by the thought of being just a housewife and mother who insists she is a writer though she never gets published, I began to see myself as an "academic" with the security of identity that an artist can never have. I decided to take reading courses after the baby was born. In three months I would return to classes. All seemed well planned. And I was more content during the last trimester than I had been for six months.

Despite my immobility in bed and huge belly, sexual pleasure had returned. Making love in my old room, I often cried, overwhelmed by the new depth my love for James had come to include. And fully believing I could do everything in this world after the baby was born, study, mother, even write again, I believed James when he said I was beautiful.

Several weeks before my due date we returned to New Haven. School was over for the summer. I had to see the doctor once a week, and in our Lamaze class the women waddled more and more uncomfortably with each session. I tried to study in the library every day, but all I ever did was time Braxten-Hicks contractions. The closer I was to delivery, the less I believed I was going to have a baby. The more bruised my belly became from kicks and pokes, the more unreal it all seemed.

Basically, for four weeks I waited. It was impossible for me to do

anything else. I would time three contractions at twenty-minute inter-
vals and then they would disappear. I looked forward to my doctor's
appointments with the eagerness of a child on the night before Christmas. I climbed eagerly onto the examination table, waiting for him to
say, "Five centimeters dilated."

Instead he always said, "Could go for another week."

I would try to force him into a commitment.

"But I might dilate eight in one night, right?" I begged.

"You might, but I doubt it."

I knew he was never wrong. In the next five days, while I waited, hot
and sweating, for the jailhouse door to open, he would probably pull
five or six slimy, gray, froglike bodies from big red holes which were
mysteriously connected to the weary faces on the other side of the
mountain. And this doctor was an older man, an experienced physi-
cian. Imagine how many big red holes and weary faces he had to keep
correctly paired in his mind. Yet I insistently expected him to see my
hole and my slimy frog as something special. Refusing to see him for
what he was, a well-trained technician, I approached each weekly examination with the same fluttering expectation I had once reserved for
my analytic sessions. But this time the receiver of all my passionate
transference could barely remember my name.

Secretly, I continued to imagine that somehow he cared about me.
When I proved my strength and psychic health in the labor room,
controlling my contractions perfectly, experiencing the easy delivery I
expected, he might even admire me. It didn't matter that I didn't particularly like him. I was impelled to create some kind of connection.

Several of my friends had told me they were sure I would have an
easy labor. I was so maternal, a veritable Earth Mother. It was my very
nature to bear children, they said, and I believed them. We were all still
locked into that vicious lie that if a woman is really a woman, she will
bear children gracefully; if she is ultimately feminine, she will mysteriously know how to be a good mother. Even after nine months of a
pregnancy which suggested that either the myth was untrue or I was a
colossal failure, I still believed the lie.

One night the pains didn't go away. At two in the morning I remembered the Lamaze teacher saying, "When you're in labor, if it's at night,
let your husband sleep. He'll need it. You can time your contractions
and wake him at the proper moment."

I woke James immediately. As soon as the pains changed dramatically, I knew I had to have him with me. I was afraid of giving birth on the bathroom floor. The tightening in my belly was already pretty intense, and I no longer knew what to expect. I grabbed my suitcase with its lollipop, washcloth (instruments of the Lamaze technique) and copy of Dr. Spock and called the doctor. I felt ready. I wondered who could have been more prepared. As we got into the car, I was grateful for the gift of reason. I would be in control.

On the way to the hospital, I started the breathing. There was a little part of me standing aside, laughing, saying, You crazy girl, don't you know you're the wrong customer for this nonsense? You'll never make yourself concentrate on something else. While the other part of me kept up the rhythmic breathing. I was sure I was nine centimeters opened.

Fifteen hours later I was lying on the bed in the labor room, a bottle of sugar water attached to my vein, still only three centimeters dilated. I had cried, vomited, tried to convince my miserable body to give forth the child. Nothing worked. All sense of unity with my body seemed to be broken. We were separated by a cement wall. But, in spite of the sleeping potion they had fed me, I was never more my unpretentious self, locked mercilessly in the burning moment of the present.

I thought of my friends who said it would be easy. But nothing had ever been easy for me. And during that whole day of pain, I continued to see myself with a clarity I would have preferred to reserve for another time.

The pains were so strong I couldn't imagine anything more being "active labor." Then everything changed. The chemically induced fog I had floated in for hours disappeared as something tore through my body. I yelled in shocked agony. I knew I couldn't get through it.

"Call my husband," I screamed when I could catch my breath. James had gone home to rest and they were rushing me to the delivery room. Apparently, when I finally started dilating I had opened six centimeters in ten minutes.

But that hint of the unpredictable, often unmanageable, nature of motherhood disappeared again as I realized that James had arrived and was standing behind me as they strapped my wrists down, draped me in green, got the gas mask ready.

And having yanked my image of mother down into my own sore body for one moment, I saw her take one look at me and float laughingly back up into the clouds.

Someone arranged the mirror so I could see my baby being born. I took one look at the huge red hole between my legs and shut my eyes tight for the rest of the delivery.

But this was my first baby, and I was determined not to be frightened. It must be all right, I thought, imagining all the women in the world who had given birth before me. I was holding back the "urge to push" as the doctor had instructed and, each time the threat of terror crept close, the modulated voices behind the masks encouraged me. Of course I knew that if I were in fact dying, no one would scream unpleasantly SHE'S DYING. Instead the same sensible, modulated tones would continue. Nevertheless, I was calmed by the pretense.

When the doctor finally told me to bear down and push I began to scream, never having imagined such monstrous pain.

"Stop screaming," he instructed. "It doesn't help anyone."

"It helps me!" I yelled with an intensity I am sure he discounted as a symptom of the psychosis often exhibited by women in transition.

But I had never been more sane. I knew only that I had to survive. I pushed hard only because that was the only way to get the bastard out. And because pushing is not an urge; it is a demand backed up by all the violence your body, turned suddenly into an enemy, has at its command.

Somewhere in the back of my mind I remembered a woman on the Lamaze record sighing ecstatically when she was told she had a boy. I knew for sure I would never be like her. And pushing with all my might, I experienced for a moment what I would feel for hours with my next child—the certainty that I was dying.

Then Benjamin was born. The pain disappeared and my social self returned to me in a flash.

"It's a boy," the doctor said.

I sighed ecstatically for the crowd in a last tribute to my shattered illusions, thinking only, Thank God it's out, thank God it's out.

Later, my white-shrouded audience gone to another woman now moaning through her own nightmare, I was alone in the recovery room. I had held my baby, looked into his eyes. I stood for a long while at the window, watching the night, blood still trickling down my legs. I was overwhelmed by my own power and endurance, weeping and laughing. I felt I had never wanted anything more than to be a mother. And I swore I would never have another child.

3

For the first eight days home Benjamin slept and ate. In the early evening, when he cried a while, my mother-in-law, Marie, would walk him, relieving our anxiety by knowing what to do. She had come from North Carolina to be with us for the first two weeks of his life. In the middle of the night, when he awoke for his feeding, I was relatively comfortable, knowing that I had only to nurse him for a half-hour and hand him back to her in case he wasn't ready to return to sleep. Still exhausted from giving birth, still bleeding heavily, I was content to spend most of the day in bed. When I felt guilty for such inactivity, imagining the women of ancient China marching out to the fields after burying the placenta, I would listen eagerly to Marie's stories of how she was kept in bed for nine days after the birth of each child. And she could not be accused of being spoiled or middle-class.

She had begun having babies when she was sixteen, and had continued having them for the next five years. By the time she was my age, the youngest of her four children was five. I thought of the convenient laundry room in the student complex where we lived. I had been shocked when, after four days of Benjamin's life, we had accumulated enough wash for three tubs. But when Marie was twenty-five, with four children running around her small apartment in a southern project, there had not even been the dream of a washing machine.

"Mama was the washing machine," I had heard my brother-in-law say.

Vaguely, I could remember my grandmother scrubbing our clothes on an old washing board before they had installed the machine in our basement. Now I pictured Marie, using the same kind of board, with four tubs of clothing lined up and waiting. And whereas I simply folded all the dry baby clothes and put them in the drawer, she ironed every-thing, down to the little undershirts. It was a sign that your babies were cleaned, cared-for, loved. The entire project would have talked about you if your children appeared in wrinkled clothes.

Listening to her tell of her own children's infancy as she took care of her grandchild, I wished for the millionth time that she had been my mother. What did I care about poverty, about racism, about the small-town boredom my husband always recalled bitterly? Hadn't her chil-dren always had a mother? Hadn't she been home with them from the day of their birth until they marched victoriously off to college? Hadn't she cooked magnificent meals and baked pies for no special occasion? Hadn't all the things I had always wanted been theirs? Never mind that Marie's youth was spent in exhausting labor for which she never re-ceived a penny. Never mind that she told me she had cried every night for years from sheer exhaustion. I wanted her for my own. And, failing that, I thought, as I watched her walk my baby up and down the living room, calming his colic with her broad shoulder, I would be a mother just like her. Her children, my husband and his sister and brothers, might think of me as a child who had everything, all of the cultural and intellectual and economic security a middle-class childhood might of-fer. But it was they who assumed the real miracle to be a simple fact of life. During those days, I was unwilling to see any of the complexities of Marie's life. She was the incarnation of the maternal myth, wiser than Dr. Spock himself. Yes. I would be like her.

A few days before she was to leave, I started to sweat. No matter how cold the room was, I was sweltering. Marie was constantly throwing blankets over Benjamin, while I was convinced he would die of heat exhaustion. And although everybody coming into the apartment con-firmed Marie's view of the temperature, I was certain that the sixty degrees registered on the thermostat was a lie. It had to be at least ninety, I insisted, as the wet drops of terror flowed over my eyes.

The day before she left, Benjamin cried unceasingly. Marie walked, rocked and patted him for hours, but he wouldn't fall asleep. When James came home from school, he hovered over the baby, trying to help his mother, or he walked Benjamin himself as Marie prepared dinner. I held back my tears, choked on the words of need trying to push them-selves out of my mouth. I hated Marie and James for worrying so much about the goddamn baby when I wanted to be held, stroked, rocked. Although it was close to feeding time and in spite of the fact that I had not been more than several feet away from the house since I had returned from the hospital, I left, slamming the door behind me.

Now Marie would know what a shrew her son had married, I thought. Now I would jeopardize her affection as my true self was exposed to her for the first time. I ran away from the little circle of houses in which the young families of Yale students could hide from the real world, the "community," which crowded toward us at the bottom of the hill. I didn't care if running increased my bleeding. Better to bleed to death on the road than risk insanity in my living room.

I ran until I could hardly breathe. I stopped at the biology building, which rose up out of a vast and beautiful field. There was no one in sight to interrupt the stately coherence of the architecture. The stark, red columns were relentlessly even; the stone balconies and geometric archways contrasted sharply with the old oaks all around and the Gothic towers in the distance. I felt soothed. The red and gray stone might be the strange creations of some far-off planet. Everything was simple, unburdened by any flourish, and I tried not to think of my living room, crowded with baby furniture and soiled receiving blankets. Here I could lie down on the cold cement path and retreat into hours of uninterrupted slumber. For ten days now my life had been divided into three-hour sections. Sleep and feed. Sleep and feed. Sleep and feed.

I had always required a lot of sleep. "A result of intense anxiety," all the articles on character neurosis said. I had learned to feel in control of my raging mind, always full of demons and intensity, by keeping perfect track of my dreams. Now, suddenly, I was not only unable to remember them, I couldn't even finish them.

I felt I should never have had a baby. If anyone had told me what it would be like, I might have saved my life in time. Who was this immensely powerful person, screaming unintelligibly, sucking my breast until I was in a state of fatigue the likes of which I had never known? Who was he and by what authority had he claimed the right to my life? I would never be a good mother. Hadn't I already caused him to be colicky with my own treacherous anxiety? The experts were right, I thought. Babies are born to be placid, contented creatures. It is only the bad mother repressing her unfair resentment, holding the baby too tightly, too loosely, too often, too rarely, letting him cry, picking him up too soon, feeding him too much, too little, suffocating him with her love or not loving him enough—it is only the bad mother who is to blame.

How, I wondered, had I ever blamed my parents for anything?

I hugged my sweater tightly around me. No belly to get in the way. Though I was still ten pounds heavier than my usual weight, I felt positively gaunt. I was so thankful not to be pregnant any more, I laughed and stroked my body which now belonged only to me once again. I might diet without worrying about fetal nutrition; I might exercise until I dropped—only I would be fatigued. Then I felt my blouse dampen with the sweet, clear milk. It was time for Benjamin to eat. I ran all the way home waiting impatiently for the feel of his smooth little cheek against my breast.

His mouth, vulnerable and innocent at other times, grabbed my nipple and sucked it into himself with a ferocity, a knowledgeability, which was awesome in its purity. I had never before been in contact with such driven instinct. After only several days of his life, we both felt that the breast was his. As he drew the milk out of me, my inner self seemed to shrink into a very small knot, gathering intensity under a protective shell, moving away, further and further away, from the changes being wrought by this child who was at once separate and a part of me. Frightened that he would claim my life completely, I desperately tried to cling to my boundaries. Yet I held him very close, stroked his skin, imagined that we were still one person.

I turned to that self inside of me, that girlwoman who had once been all I needed to know of myself, whom I had fought to understand, to love, to free—I turned to her now and I banished her. Into a protective shell tied in a knot, she retreated, four, five, six times a day, whenever Benjamin wanted to nurse. Soon, even when I sought her, she would not come, but began to stay out of reach longer and longer, sometimes not reappearing for whole days. For if she was present when the baby needed me, she was of necessity pushed aside, sent to go hungry. She who had been my life, whom I knew I had to nourish daily in order to be fed in return, hid for weeks, hoarding her gentleness and her strength, placing no gifts in my outstretched hands.

In my arms, I held my baby. After he drank from me, sometimes he would sleep. I stayed still for hours then, staring at his face, comparing his toes to mine, finding a turn of his mouth which reminded me of my sister's, discovering in the shape of his torso the suggestion of his father's body. Every detail of his face seemed, like a photograph taken many years before, to ring with the tones of my own features. I was always looking for something familiar, a prospector searching for a treasure which would set the world right.

At other times, during and after feedings, he would cry and scream. I would walk him through the house, weeping with him for my incompetence, apologizing for my anxious and jittery soul, which was clearly the wrong style for good mothers. Sometimes I hated him for rejecting me so completely; "Shut up! I'll kill myself if you don't shut up!" I'd yell. Then I would try to shove my nipple into his mouth and he would push it away, his face distorted with pain.

I'd put him in the carriage so as not to harm him with my tentacles of rage, and I'd sit huddled on the couch, door slammed unsuccessfully against his cries, holding my ears and moaning with loss. And in the corner of my desk, my typewriter and my record books sat silently, mocking me through layers of dust.

When he had cried long enough to subdue my anger, I held him and rocked him again until he became quiet. I checked his breathing, kissed his lips, his eyes, warding off the spirit of psychosis and, mercifully, he was willing to suck. I held him close as our dark eyes met, telling him silently, Suck, darling, take me, use me to grow. Live, My Life, and love me, love me, while I try desperately to love you.

4

On the inevitable afternoon that Marie boarded the bus for home, James and I walked back to our apartment, joking about our fear. But the next morning the jokes were stale. James went to school, and for the first time in the two weeks of his life, Benjamin and I faced the morning alone together. I tried to remember Marie's advice; how to carry him on my shoulder when he was upset. But without her constant stories and memories filling up my sedentary days, my ignorance seemed infinite and I walked headlong into my suddenly solitary life.

But the truth was that I was not solitary, not merely alone. Instead I was isolated, lonely, the way I had been many years before, long before I had begun to write. In those days the moment I found myself without company I would rush to turn the radio on, hoping it would drown out the discomforting thoughts, or I would reach desperately for the telephone, calling anyone who might be home. Since I had begun writing, I had sought time alone. That very self I had once sought to flee, who had hovered around me like a claw-sharpened dragon threatening to invade my body and claim it for its own, that dangerous, frightening self was precisely what I had learned to treasure, what I had begun to learn to understand.

That was the trouble, perhaps. I had only begun. It was still possible for the dangerous self to remain outside and become the dragon again, ominously trying to invade. In order to tame it, I had to write, regularly and consistently, and in order to write I had to be alone.

Now suddenly I was always with Benjamin. I was still in some physical pain from giving birth. Emotionally I walked a tightrope of passions. Only when he slept did my sense of aloneness approximate my former experience, and since he slept most peacefully outside, that is where I usually was.

Prospect Street was tree-lined in a way which was mythical to a New Yorker. Pushing Benjamin's carriage down the black asphalt hill, through all the golden browns and stark oranges of New Haven's autumn, I watched the trees with the same shock I have seen on the faces of the tourists in New York: they walk up Broadway from Ninety-sixth Street, aghast at the mentally and physically disabled lining the sidewalks who lean out of their wheelchairs, dirty, twisted palms thrust before your eyes, demanding a quarter, or nod in a drug-saturated heaven right in the middle of the street, daring the speeding cars to hit their tortured bodies, exhibiting a last life-saving ounce of pride and defiance. The tourists are silent, but their eyes whisper, Can this be real?

I am a New Yorker; I am more used to the homeless and junkies than I am to breath-taking autumn leaves going on and on and on, never stopping until you can't see any longer, down the road.

I found my inner girlwoman during those walks. I began to take my record book with me, stopping every so often to record an emotion instead of allowing it to slip silently away. In the space created by the silence of both of our voices, I found my deep, welling, absolutely immutable love for my son.

After several weeks of the same road, and the same trees, the call of the city drummed out the pleasant sound of leaves crackling under my feet. I began to keep walking until I was downtown, in the midst of the university I watched the natives of a world I had suddenly lost going about their important business, looking involved, busy, even rushed. While I had all the time in the world.

I walked toward the law school, longing for a smile of grown-up recognition from someone, anyone, who was over three weeks old. Rocking the carriage, although by now Benjamin was in a deep sleep, I waited for my husband. James, no longer simply my lover and friend, had become that conventional, adult-sounding thing—my husband. And I, who had come to New Haven only because James was in school here, who knew no one except his fellow students, his friends, whose own life, furthermore, had been turned upside down by permanent changes, I was "Jim's wife." So I was known and so I was called. Even to my face.

"Oh, so you're Jim's wife," I would hear many times. Which is not entirely offensive if you are standing firmly upon the solid ground of your own identity. I, on the other hand, was slithering in and out of the muck of self-doubt at a velocity which was steering me toward the rim of hysteria.

So I was pleased when some of the women law students approached me one day, not only remembering me, but wondering expectantly when I would feel well enough to join their recently organized women's liberation group which they hoped would substitute for the "Wives Association"—that traditional appendage to every graduate school. This new group was open to all women connected to the law school—students, wives of students, secretaries and professors. But since the only woman professor at the law school did not choose to come, and none of the secretaries was interested, the group comprised students and wives of students. I was disgusted to find myself in the latter category. No matter that I was a student at another school in New York. My category was determined by my relationship to Yale. And to Yale I was and always will be a "student wife."

Still, I decided to give some thought to joining the group. I was certainly in favor of replacing the "Wives Association" with something more meaningful.

When we had arrived in New Haven a year before, someone from the Law Wives Association had called me.

"Hello," said the pleasant midwestern voice on the phone. I swore not to be an eastern snob, tried to forget that I was a swarthy Jew and my husband an even swarthier Black. She had called me to invite me to an association meeting.

"What do you do?" I tried feeling open as a flower in the spring. Why shouldn't she be a vital, intelligent future friend?

"We have clubs."

"Clubs?" I whispered weakly.

"Yes." She was, I could tell, about to lay the climax on me. "We have many interests. There are sewing, cooking, wine-tasting which sometimes gets pretty hairy, law school business because our husbands never tell us anything." She giggled.

I responded with a strange, animal-like grunt.

"What are your interests?" she finished sweetly.

"Mostly I read, and write. Politics," I said abruptly.

"Oh, we don't get too political, but we do have a literary club." She was expectant.

I, standing at the crossroads between intolerant rudeness and self-defeating falsity, was silent.

"And it is a wonderful way to make friends," she courted.

"Well, no, perhaps we'll meet somewhere else . . . " I tried to keep what I know can be an edgy condescension out of my voice.

"Let us just send you our flyers then . . . "

Why was she so persistent? What did she want with me? Why was my lack of interest in her so unacceptable? Perhaps the whispers of liberation, those words which would sound so true as to become quickly trite, were already in the air of her house as well as mine. Perhaps she realized somehow that within one year the Law Wives Association, having carried hundreds of young women through an otherwise meaningless, lonely three years of watching their husbands go to school, having given them at least someone to talk to, would be wiped off the law school activity slate with not so much as a "pleasant to have met you" and replaced by the Law Women's Association, an off-shoot of the growing women's liberation consciousness-raising group which met every Sunday night in the meeting room of a local radical organization.

Several weeks after the phone call, I heard that a women's liberation group was being formed and rushed to a meeting. Finally, I thought, I will be able to translate my political values into some sort of concrete action. I looked forward to the Sunday night meetings with the eagerness I had once reserved for Saturday night dates. At our first meeting we agreed that our commitment to Sunday night would become a priority in our lives. If we were away for the weekend, we would return in time for the meeting; we would accept no social engagements; no dates with men would interfere. And this discipline was exhilarating because it accepted and sought to correct an emotional reality: in the past, women had always sacrificed obligations to other women if the needs of a man interfered. Heterosexuality, or its promise, was ever an unquestionable priority, a priority which we were now attempting to reverse. And we did. Very few women ever missed a meeting. We each spoke in turn, going around in a circle to avoid the usual domination of the most articulate.

Sharing was at the bottom of our happiness, sharing histories and feelings with other women. Isolation was what we would destroy. Communality in all of life was our goal. None of us was that different from the others: that was the great realization. Our relationships, our fears, our orgasms—everything was wonderfully the same. We threw out our make-up and sought anonymous refuge in dungarees and T-shirts. We exchanged delicate slippers for comfortable work shoes.

In high school, during the early days of the civil rights movement, I had known the pride of walking down the street in the appropriate costume. My black tights and dirty sneakers would announce to all that I believed in equality. My hair parted down the middle and pulled over my ears would further suggest my commitment to integration, and the deep blue of my pea jacket would finally confirm the flaming red of my politics. Yes. Uniform was important.

Now our clothing was related even more intimately to our values. And before the magazines and television announcers and then our vulnerable American selves degraded it into one more dictatorial fashion, the new uniform was truly a suit of liberation. I will always understand the beauty of the simple gray Chinese suit worn by both men and women. In transitional stages in history, aesthetic flamboyance is gladly sacrificed for the freedom from stereotyping and flaunted sexuality which an attractive uniformity can provide.

Over were the years of squeezing swollen feet into size six shoes, of wearing ballet slippers in the rain because they were more graceful than boots, of sitting interminably cross-legged, of pulling my mini-skirts down over underpants. I moved broadly and luxuriously in my loose dungarees and cotton shirt, amazed and relieved that I no longer attracted the eyes of every man on the street.

I fought many battles with James but, before we had children, the justice of most feminist positions was obvious to him. As a Black child, he had been brought up to believe that too much weakness in anyone was lethal. He had always been attracted to strong women, and he certainly understood the importance of details in the politics of liberation. We would be compatriots; our vision of the future was androgynous. Then I became pregnant.

By the last months of pregnancy, I had withdrawn from my friends in the movement, had lost the nourishing sense of relatedness. As other women sat comfortably with their legs astride, I was reacquainted with concern about people looking up my skirt; for my belly, by that time, precluded dungarees. Though I hated my maternity dresses, heavily laden with bows and little birds sitting comfortably atop nests, the demands of comfort made me reach eagerly for those flowered relics each morning. It was July, I was always drenched in sweat, I needed my legs bare.

I was the only woman in the group who would be a mother. Early in my pregnancy, I had become aware of a discomforting sense of dependency on James. We could no longer go our separate ways as simply if love ran dry. And I waited eagerly each night for him to walk in the door, knowing for at least one more evening that I would care for my young in relative security.

But this feeling of dependency was incomprehensible to women who had never been pregnant. As they spoke confidently of politics and their work, fear gathered in my throat and muffled my words. I wanted to shout—I may never work again.

For the first time in my life I could not speak about my feelings. I wondered if I would ever think of anything but my child again. My friends told me of back packs and assured me that they would baby-sit while I worked; I suspected it would not be true. They didn't understand, nor did I have the courage to explain, that I did not fear not being able to work again so much as never wanting to work again.

Before my mother went to work in the mornings and the maid came to take care of me, I would sit on the floor and transfer all the things from the red bag, worn yesterday with the black dress, to the navy bag, worn today with the navy dress. Then I would be allowed to choose a flower, a scarf, or some other accessory for her to wear on her coat. She was beautiful—so everyone said. And I remembered her that way. I remembered her clothes. She had been buried, they told me, in her most beautiful dress—the one with blue velvet lining the collar and cuffs, the one I had always pinned the artificial pink rose upon. That dress was dust by now. And having permanently confused her final leaving in the expensive blue velvet dress with all those other leavings when I wanted her to stay, I swore I would never leave my baby with a stranger.

I was becoming the mother I had been seeking for twenty years. My former ambitions seemed paltry. I stopped going to meetings and did not return to the group where I was the only mother in the room.

Now, walking back and forth to and from the law school, I thought more and more about joining this new women's group which might possibly include both halves of my painfully divided self. I still considered myself a feminist, but being a mother was consuming my life. Lately I had spent a lot of time talking with the other mothers in the student housing project where we lived. Many of them were from the Midwest, and had never spoken to a Black or even a Jew before. They were terrified of asking their husbands to help with the children. I could not talk to them of any of the subjects which interested me; I was even embarrassed to say I was in graduate school for fear of appearing a snob; these women had quit college to have their first babies years before.

But they were mothers. I talked continually about the merits of diapers over Pampers, when to start solids, how to calm colic, how to space nursing, how to sense the feelings behind Benjamin's impenetrable wails. I concentrated on their advice, knowing all the time that I could never be like them. As I had done since childhood, I coped with my loneliness by feasting on it, clutching it around me in the mad hope that if it was all there was to life, I could at least diminish its power by loving it. For to be lonely was at least to be something. I left the court only to go for a walk or to buy groceries. I sat and stared at Benjamin. I slept with the intensity of the interred. I hid.

About a mile down the road, Bobby Seale and Ericka Huggins were sitting in their prison cells.

One day James came home with a leaflet announcing a mass demonstration to be held on the Green demanding their release. The newspapers were filled with somber predictions of violence. In town, storekeepers started boarding up their windows. Yale undergraduates sent their stereos home for safekeeping. Everyone expected riots. In the court where we lived, the frightened families began packing up their children to send to grandparents, while Benjamin's grandfather, my father, began making plans to come to New Haven for the demonstration. It had been ten years since he had ceased functioning as a full-time revolutionary, but during those years, he had taken the train to Harlem in order to be on the scene for the ghetto rebellion; he had taken the train to Newark when that city had become a battlefield; he had probably attended every peace demonstration between Boston and Philadelphia since the protest against the war in Viet Nam began. Now he would come to New Haven.

Until now, we had encountered racism only as an inadvertent ignorance, at worst an indiscretion. In the hospital when Benjamin was born, the Black nurses and a few of the whites had dealt with us in politely correct anger. But most of the white nurses seemed frightened; when they held Benjamin I noticed the same fear lurking around the edges of their faces as I had seen in other white faces, in town, in stores, in our housing complex, when they spoke of Bobby Seale. They knew he was locked up and safely away from them, but somehow he had invaded their world, placed one foot tentatively but irreversibly upon their security. What would happen when he was released? What if there was a demonstration?

With Benjamin—who was so tiny his name hadn't stuck yet, so we still called him "the baby"—with Benjamin, they were similarly threatened. Blacks were acceptable to these democratic New Englanders—in their own world, or even coming over to the white world to visit. Whites worked with Black nurses, even under Black doctors. *Blacks.* They were, if not completely understood, at least recognizable. But here, concretized irrefutably before their eyes, lying comfortably in their knowledgeable arms, was that creature who has stalked the white nightmare for all of American history, born at times of transcendant love, at others of twisted desire, a creature who threatens the boundaries we have drawn around ourselves—the hybrid.

Still, like any other newborn, he shit black meconium and those well-disciplined nurses put aside their hatred, their wonder or whatever it was that caused their cheeks to tighten when they entered my room, and relieved my anxiety, assuring me that he was not bleeding internally. They diapered him when I sat in fear of the lethal power of the safety pin. And when he screamed so loud that I imagined him to be at death's door, they laughed at him, congratulating him on the power of his lungs. They dubbed him "Little Black Panther," trying undauntingly to place him in a familiar category, saying silently to that little pale face and those bluish eyes, You are Black. And I smirked condescendingly when they caught my eye.

Several days later, in the court where we lived, a woman had suggested that I didn't have to protect my baby from the sun as he was "black." Another neighbor insisted with a driven assurance that she had seen James downtown when I knew he had spent the whole day in his room studying. But she had seen a Black man and she would not believe it had not been James. One night I was mugged in the driveway to the court and, as James ran out to help me, hearing my screams from our living room, the police who were sirening into the driveway almost arrested him.

Now the fear of Blacks was stark, intense, unembarrassed. The women began forming groups to discuss protection from the Black hordes they expected to swarm up the hill, raping and kidnaping as they came. They assigned their men to guard duty during the weekend of the demonstration.

I was relieved that we would march in the demonstration. It would be the first time since Benjamin's birth that I would leave the house for something unrelated to my baby or housework. Besides, since the days of my childhood I had never lost my passion for mass demonstrations.

When many people of the left, discouraged by failure, began staying home from the yearly peace marches of the sixties, I waited impatiently every spring for the morning when we would gather at Union Square before dawn to board the buses for Washington. On several of those occasions, I had marched with my father and the other Veterans of the Spanish Civil War. We all laughed good-naturedly as the aging comrades joked with each other about their white hair, grandchildren tagging after them, wrinkled fingers clasped around the poles of the fraying banners proudly announcing the Veterans of the Abraham Lincoln Brigade. We cried as the crowds lining the curb applauded and shouted, paying respectful tribute to an old, magnificent moment of glory. And I moved happily beneath the comfortable cloak of my father's identity.

Our generation had not sent a volunteer brigade to North Viet Nam. If we had, I am sure I would not have gone. Is it just a different time or is it a less loving heart? Is it that, condemned to wonder relentlessly whether the future will bring compassion or murder, I have nothing to die for? Or is it that war has been the province of men, so that this was where my father, with whom I had always identified, and I finally parted ways? I was left only with the certainty that I had to bear witness, that at least it was necessary to shout.

So when Benjamin was one month old, James and I pushed him down to the Green for his first demonstration, a sign demanding that Bobby and Ericka be freed pasted to his carriage.

"Maybe we shouldn't have brought him," I said to James, thinking of the promises of violence that had filled the newspapers for weeks. The government forces were prepared for war while the organizers of the demonstration insisted the day would be peaceful. My father whistled softly as we passed the army jeeps and trucks which filled the roads as we came closer to the crowded Green. Soldiers stood seriously, their rifles readied on their shoulders. I was aghast. I didn't know whether to run or laugh. I had never been so close to guns before, nor to young men who seemed to actually believe they might shoot them.

Over and over in the last year, as the truths of the women's movement burrowed into my brain, forming ridges of knowledge which never again would be smoothed over by pleasantries, I had thought, This really is a man's world.

"I've never been afraid of a woman on a dark street," said Kate Millett at a conference I had attended. And I realized suddenly that if not for men I would be able to travel the world freely, without fear of violent attack.

One year before, I would have looked at those armed boys staring stubbornly past all our eyes, and seen only soldiers; I would have felt connected to all of the people who had come to New Haven, armed with passion and leaflets, to face the guns. I would certainly have felt completely at one with James, my father and my new son. Now, though I walked closer to them, knew we were feeling many of the same things, I also felt apart from them. In some small and strange way they were closer to those soldiers than I was. They were part of the game. I was the wife, the daughter, who would be left behind as they marched off to war, who would mourn as their bodies were splattered into the sky. They might do fierce battle with the enemy in the ring, but I was way on the other side of the fence. They were men and I was part of womenandchildren. The world, in all its wonder and horror, seemed to belong more to my tiny son, sleeping in his carriage, than it did to me. I had no desire, as did some other women I knew, to see young girls standing alongside the olive-green boys, averting their eyes from the jolt of seeing a target turn suddenly into a human face. Yet I felt myself to be a guest in the world, following the rules written out for my sex, not wanting to obey them, but seeing nothing more desirable in the world of violence inhabited by men. My father and James were here to march for peace. Yet I sensed an acceptance of the violence they abhorred, a comfort at least with its existence. I wondered if I would be able to protect my son from a fascination with that masculine reality.

We were standing in the middle of the thousands of people now, but I saw only the faces of the women in the crowd. The men had all lost their individuality and blended into two masses of color—olive green for the soldiers, blue denim for the demonstrators. I looked hard at James's face, wishing I might lock my eyes into his, see only his gentleness. I stared into my father's blue eyes, remembered his face when I had graduated from public school, when I had stayed awake all night with him, trying not to scratch my measles, when I handed him his grandchild for the first time. I bent down to kiss Benjamin's eyes, dark now with lashes grown black and thick, and let my lips move all over his soft face.

I moved a few feet away as the speeches began, off to myself. James and I had already fought over his responsibility to share care of the baby. Now I saw that it would be much more complicated than writing a schedule of duties. And I was not surprised when after each speech the crowd yelled, FREE BOBBY, and some of the speakers forgot to mention that Ericka Huggins was in prison too.

I determined to recommit myself to feminism. Other women had been mothers without sacrificing ambition and political ideals—so why not me? I would go to the next meeting of the women's liberation group at the law school where there would be other mothers in the room. Walking back from the demonstration, waiting for the guns which would shake the night, I felt the first relief from my long period of loneliness, the relief which accompanies a sense of belonging, no matter how temporary or even false that sense might be. Somewhere on the fringe of the men's revolution there was a spot called the "women's movement." It was there that I would sit comfortably again and find ways of changing the world, there that I would escape for a while the transformation of my loved solitude into isolation. Through feminism I would seek community in social action. Perhaps I would carry my baby on my back after all, and my sisters would help me care for him, obliterating the terrible choice which always confronted me in the truth-saturated middle of the night between self-sacrifice and strange baby-sitters. I would go to a meeting, walk proudly into the room where I was known already as a local feminist: like my father before me, I would be an organizer.

For several days, in anticipation of the meeting, I coped efficiently and maturely with the difficulties of my life. I was a gentle mother. I found small unconnected stretches of time to read and write in my record books. The mask of "Jim's wife" began to slip off my face.

I had carefully tucked extra tissues in my bra so that leaking milk would be quickly absorbed. Even though there were other mothers in the Law Women's Association, I was embarrassed by the possibility of so unsubtle a sign of maternity. Of course the women in the law school knew I had just had a baby, were waiting to congratulate me; still, when my friend honked the horn in the driveway and I turned to leave the house, even though it had taken me over five minutes to leave painfully detailed instructions for my husband—what to do if the baby should wake, if he should wet, if he should choke, where to find me at every moment if he rejected the bottle—still, the very instant I walked out the door, knowing that I could no longer hear Benjamin's cry, I began to pretend I did not have a baby. For that one minute that it took me to walk down the steps toward the waiting car, the girlwoman filled me almost to breathlessness.

I felt the night differently than I had in several weeks, with no little bundle in my arms, no carriage marching like a demanding and powerful master before me. I saw the stars differently, seeing them as I did quite alone, staring only at them instead of averting my eyes constantly to see whether Benjamin continued to sleep peacefully. I stood outside the car, drinking in the aloneness, breathing it into my lungs, cutting off for a splendid second my connection to my body which in every way reminded me of my new status, retrieving in that second my familiar self which was not yet altogether lost.

The scar from my episiotomy stretched painfully as I sat down and I had to move gingerly onto the side of my buttocks so as not to put pressure on my hemorrhoids. My breasts were heavy, filled with excesses of milk, and I winced as I leaned over to receive my friend's congratulatory kiss. I answered her inevitable questions about the experience of giving birth as briefly as possible, for it was not easy to leap out of the quiet, dark, velvet world in which I had stood alone for a moment.

Fifteen minutes later, as we walked into the law school, I thought about the students and the wives of students who would be meeting each other tonight. I wondered how two such different groups of women would get along together. The law students were, by any conventional standard, the most successful achievers of their generation of women. Most had gone to the best Ivy League women's schools in the country. They had resisted, thus far, the pull of marriage, not to mention motherhood. Not only were they preparing to be lawyers, a traditionally "masculine" profession, but they had been accepted by the best law school in the country before women had put pressure on admissions committees. Thus, as women who had individually overcome the substantial prejudice against them in the world of professional and graduate training, they, like the nine or ten Blacks who had arrived that fall, were probably among the most intelligent and qualified students in the entire class.

Those ambitious, self-confident, successful women had to be very different people from the wives, I thought, as we walked through the dim, oak hallways. These were women who had fallen in love early, several already had more than one child. Others worked to support their husbands' education. One year before, they would have been members of the Law Wives Association, forcing themselves to appear interested in the clubs, trying to reach past the façades of literary interest and the exchange of recipes into the hearts of the other wives, so that they might rest a moment from the burden of being cooks, maids, confidantes, secretaries, mistresses, mothers and daughters to their husbands, and talk frankly to other women. In fact, most wives of students had chosen to remain in the still functioning Wives Association. Only a brave few had come to this women's liberation group, full of fears of facing their more successful sisters who were among the favorite children of the new feminist movement. I was one of the wives. But I felt no more connection to them than I did to the students. As usual, I thought wryly, whether by comfortable choice or temperament, I was like a swimmer who is caught with a cramp equally far from the raft and shore, floundering somewhere in between. I sat, however, on the couch where most of the wives had gathered.

As someone suggested that we begin, the students leaned slightly forward and the wives leaned slightly back; it was up to the students to insist, from their comfortable perch of clear superiority, that we were all sisters.

Some of them sprawled in a relaxed sort of way on the beautiful wooden floor carpeted with an old Oriental rug. One student curled up in a vast red leather chair without even taking off her shoes. Another woman rested her feet casually on an old wooden coffee table whose price, I couldn't help imagining, ran in the hundreds of dollars. But I sat stiffly on an expensive couch as if I expected it to eject me in a burst of upper-class assertion. Also, I was protecting my hemorrhoids. I folded my arms gracelessly over my bosom, which was bursting with milk, dampening the blouse which an hour before I had thought made me appear slim and unmaternally attractive.

Feeling about as liberated as a caged lion, I comforted myself with the reminder that, in any case, the one thing which made me different from the other wives in the eyes of the students was the fact that my husband was Black. It seemed that within these walls which sagged with the weight of history and boasted every few feet a dark-toned portrait of some illustrious juror, I was, even to my own eyes, "Jim's wife." And how comforting that was; how fortunate that his Blackness saved me from the full poisonous strength of an otherwise completely ordinary middle-class conventionality. And how relieving that the racial status of my child lent a touch, however false, of the exotic to the experience of motherhood, which throughout history has been considered to be of the utmost banality, demanding only the most mechanical, instinctual, biological response.

Only the act of giving birth seemed interesting, I knew, to the intelligent, independent young women facing me. Once that dramatic moment of creation was over, however, the image of motherhood took on, in their minds, hues of graying diapers and red-and-white gingham; they thought of unattractive housedresses, disorderly homes, interrupted careers, diminishing sexuality—with these miserable consequences wrapped in the most unobjective, uncritical, sentimental and enervating kind of love. They thought of lives which were uninteresting, conventional, over. And so did I.

I envied their brown leather briefcases left casually all around the floor, their messy hair which they'd had no time to brush since morning, busy as they were with crucial matters, their comfortable disregard for their incomparably expensive surroundings, a disregard which could only come from years of familiarity. And I envied the familiarity each seemed to feel with herself. They were young women students who, having just graduated from elite colleges, were now attending an elite law school. My desire was not for membership in their intellectual aristocracy, although that was tantalizing, so much as that secure sense of themselves which they projected, at least on the surface, which said, Yes. I know who I am. I do not need to travel deep into my soul every night and wonder who in the world I have become. I do not need to look at my law texts as you look at your child, and grow dizzy with the uncertainty of what this experience will do to my world. I do not fear, in the social company of famous men or in rising to speak in the classroom, that my own inadequacy shines in my eyes like those trick candles that will not burn out no matter how hard you blow but, maddeningly, keep lighting up again. Whatever inadequacy I feel can be hidden, covered, efficiently and effectively, with a list of my academic achievements which are there on my transcript, filed in the office, for anyone to see. So if you wives feel that you are more beautiful, more feminine, more fulfilled than we are—perhaps you are in a way. But we are the compatriots of men. We are their equals. We are the strong, the adventurous, the dynamic. You are mothers and wives.

Such were the sisterly thoughts which filled my head as I gazed over at the other couch and at the graceful bodies strewn across the floor. For they were what I had always wanted to be.

And, was I imagining it, or were the other wives sharing my hatreds and fears? Weren't their shoulders a bit too rounded, their voices too soft? Wasn't their hair too well combed and their make-up too perfectly applied, suggesting, as was the truth, that they had prepared for this evening by bathing, dressing, waiting anxiously for the moment to leave the house and the children and the husband? While the students, judging by their wrinkled clothes and tired appearance, had obviously run to this meeting straight from a demanding day. They most likely hadn't even eaten yet. After the meeting, as I headed wearily home to bed so that the two-o'clock feeding would not find me in the deepest early hours of sleep, they would all go to dinner, have a drink, and return, perhaps, to bed with men whose hands had never before touched their bodies, whose tongues would move hungrily toward their wet, pulsing vaginas. Whereas I had not felt one moment of sexual excitement since my baby had been born.

In those weeks of sexual disinterest, when I was suddenly no longer pregnant, I understood something which strangely and eerily modified the image I had for a long time carried around of myself, which I was always told I presented to others. I was an "Earth Mother," they told me, exuding receptivity. And to some degree, it may have been true. But there was something truer, something which had to do with a part of myself which was always frustrating me by remaining hidden despite my conscious attempts to express it. It kept hidden because it was frightened, frightened of its own power. For it was like those strong colors which, when mixed with gallons of white paint, change the white suddenly to a color with only the tiniest drop. If more than a drop is let out at a time, the paint is ruined; it is no longer a subtle pastel shade of pink, beige or lavender, appropriate for an aesthetically designed room, but a dark, screaming, overly dramatic red or purple.

Pregnancy and childbirth had exposed that power, made it impossible for me ever to deny it again. There it was: I had created a child. The emotional intensity I had always experienced and which was considered excessive under normal conditions, was allowed during pregnancy. Suddenly I had a right to my extremes. Controls broke dangerously away and parts of myself which others thought new and strange emerged.

After Benjamin was born I tried over and over to deny my weariness, my pain and my increasing madness by cooking dinner or vacuuming the house, trying to abandon myself to the detailed demands of everyday life. I was minimizing my experience, refusing to respect it. But each time I retreated to my bed for three more hours of interrupted, dream-filled sleep—a much too intimate meeting with my deepest self. As I wandered my way through long, solitary days, in that apparent inactivity, I was courting and accepting the truth I had been trying to deny.

Would I be able to share this truth I had grasped with the other mothers in this women's group? I wondered, scanning the faces, searching for someone whose glance or style promised the possibility of future intimacy. Might one of the students understand the transformations I was hurtling through, the realization I had had?

It was the pain, the intolerable agonizing pain of the last stages of labor that I sought to remember each time I closed my eyes, that I ached to recapture. Not for some simple, twisted desire to suffer. It was the enormity of it that drew me; I had created a child. It was the infinite mystery of it trapped unbelievably in fifteen concrete seconds that enveloped me. I was obsessed with that excruciating, uncivilized, powerful moment of birth, imprisoned like a Van Gogh in a frame in the sterile white and green delivery room which was dotted by the fatigued faces of the nurses and doctors who wanted to get home to bed. I was in the grip of a loving fascination with my own power. And I was incapable of sexual response. Only the feelings of friendship for James, an altogether new kind of closeness, were mine. But it was not to my baby's mouth that my sexual energy had gone. That was only the symbol, the living memory of the original moment of our unity and parting. My sexuality, dripping blood and embracing something quite distinct from desire, was swirling madly, unreachable, involved only with myself.

The meeting proceeded wearily around me, but I did not participate, realizing I could not explain such extreme feelings to women I hardly knew. It was quite some time until I saw that it was almost over, and I had heard very little. Guilty, thinking my reticence might be interpreted as the indifference it truly was, I spoke up more toward the end, trying, as if sticking a collage on paper with insufficient paste, to transfer to this group the insights I had learned in the passionate evenings of the first group. It was false. The students lived in a world which was miles away from my own. The other mothers had passed the period of crisis I was living through, and if their experience has been as wracking as mine, they weren't talking.

One of the mothers in the group called me at home one morning. Benjamin had not slept well for five nights. Every evening just as James and I sat down to dinner, Benjamin would commence his "period of irritable crying," shrieking in clear agony for three hours. We would take turns walking him, rocking him, singing to him, but usually nothing worked. The three hours had to pass miserably and then, exhausted, he would fall asleep for a while. For most of the interminable day while James was in school, I would walk Benjamin again, trying to quiet his pain.

"Isn't being a mother the most wonderful thing you have ever done?" the woman asked me that morning on the phone.

"Not really," I answered, holding back tears. "Actually it is quite miserable and exhausting," and I put my hand over my mouth so I would stop before it was too late.

"Oh, don't say that," she said maturely.

So I didn't. And I stopped going to the group. I was becoming convinced that I was the only mother in the world who had such hateful feelings for the child I loved so intensely, who wished over and over that it had never happened, who, finally, could understand those women I had met when working for the Welfare Department who had burnt their babies' arms, beat their faces, killed them. But I would never breathe a word of such vicious identification, I decided. I would hide my real feelings in order to avoid the terrible looks which say, I am not like you nor have I ever been.

5

Morning comes early, around five o'clock now, and it is time for the feeding. Smells of yellowish, milky shit fill his room and I clean him, kissing his incomparably soft, just-out-of-sleep face. While I hold him curled into my breasts and stomach he is quiet but when I lay him down on the cold plastic to change his diaper he becomes purple with rage and misery and, frightened that he will suffocate himself on his own cries, I rush to finish quickly, causing pains in my shoulders, which are now my constant companions as they were so long ago. Pains of anger which cannot be expressed. Pains which came after fighting with my father and which come now from living with my son. Dry and clean, he bites my neck, searching, searching for the part of me he knows so well, and finally I sit down, lean my head back and feel him suck.

All of this before even one cup of coffee.

Unlike the babies I have read about in Drs. Spock and Gesell, Benjamin does not return to sleep after nursing but remains awake and fidgety until around ten. At eight James awakens and by nine he is gone. Ten, eleven, twelve, one, two, three, I count. Six hours until he returns. I bathe Benjamin to relax him. He sinks into the water in the tub as he once did in me. It is warm. I stroke his body, it is incredibly magnificent; I smooth it with soap and run water gently over him again and again. Dry and relaxed now, he will remain quiet in his carriage near the window for perhaps twenty minutes while I have coffee.

The radio sings, "Smile a Little Smile for Me," and I walk up and down the living room holding him again, moving rhythmically for him; the next is my favorite, "Get Together," which reminds me of the union songs of my childhood. I pass by the mirror, noticing Benjamin's eyes are not yet closed; I move to the Yiddish songs my father often sang. I am pronouncing the words all wrong but I have the music right; *s'nakht in droysn*, I sing, and over and over I sing the words, *nit keyn mame*, which he sang so plaintively and beautifully sitting on our beds for hours at night after she died. For the thousandth time since Benjamin's birth I weep for her. And now, having relaxed myself with my grief, I have put him to sleep. I lay him in his carriage as slowly as a minute hand descending and tiptoe into the other room.

By then it is sometimes noon and often it is even later. But once he is asleep I love him for his intensity and for his difficulty in adjusting to life and for his pain, which are all so like my own. And when I look into his eyes I see myself and my mother and feel that he is my continuance.

In the child-care books it says not to overidentify with your baby and I have even read a case in one of Bettelheim's books about a child who was abandoned to the silence of autism by a mother who unconsciously believed the child to be herself. Terrified, I swear to stop.

At night, when James returns, I am angry with my baby. For I want James for myself and so does Benjamin. And Benjamin, like my sister before him, wins every time. I damn him and feel that I have lost everything, James being everything to me. I yell into his little face for his endless crying and throw him roughly into his crib. Then I quickly sweep him into my arms, protecting him from his insane mother, fearing that I will, of all ironic results of my own pain-filled struggle for health, drive my child crazy. For, if I interpret the experts correctly, that is not a hard thing to do.

It is not long before James becomes better than I at rocking Benjamin to sleep after I convince him that I am just as confused as he is when it comes to infants and carry no magical knowledge within me about mothering, at least it has not yet shown itself. Then I am punished for my incompetence by having to watch James hold him all evening, watch from across the room as I once watched my father hold the baby while I was far away. I have been driven back to lonely moment after lonely moment by this child, to all the moments I had thought I had learned to understand, to forgive, to banish. Instead, I cry out in rage at my fickle father whom, dangerously, James has become. I am ever-lastingly grateful that I am nursing my baby because, if not for that, what could I give him? James's shoulder is broader, his heart calmer, so he can quiet him faster, except when I really put my mind to it. James is loving and good, like his mother. My son needs them, not me. And by the time I have reached this point in the course of my thoughts, she, my own dead, damnably unreachable mother, comes crashing into my head, reminding me that she has left me forever. I too will sacrifice; I will leave my baby to more competant hands, I decide. Thus I will prove my feminism, for who said that the mother is the best caretaker of the child? Thus I will escape the shoulder pains and the fatigue and the ringing in my ears. Thus I will repay James and Benjamin for not loving me.

One night I began to pack my bag, screaming at them that I have to leave in order to prove my love. I have pushed and pushed at James's protective armor behind which he is hidden at these moments, hating the calm face and the coping soul. He is reasonable, telling me I am upset and Benjamin needs me. He is, as always, silent while I scream. I keep it up, trying to find words to hurt him with, trying to beat down his solid and trustworthy controls, ignoring how much I have loved them.

When I lock the suitcase James begins to cry, and he keeps right on crying for several hours. Amazed, I stand back and notice that he loves me. And while I hold him and stroke him and understand, now calmer and saner, that I do not have to leave, that I may stay with my baby, and while I cry for the pain I have caused in my selfish demand for assurance, I smile to myself. I have won. Perhaps that has been the point all along. But I realize that night what a gentle and vulnerable man James is.

I knew I had to begin leaving Benjamin with someone else, but I had not found a sitter, had not looked for fear of finding one. I could leave Benjamin only with James. So I went to the library once a week. On that day I did not study. I sat in the divinity school library, high up on a balcony where I had my own little wooden table next to an oval window, and I looked at the trees. I saw them change from orange and red to brown, spread thickly before me as lush as I could have imagined. Slowly I saw them grow bare. Each week I would return to my spot and watch the trees. I listened to the quiet. I felt the contours of my body and knew where I ended. Sometimes I closed my eyes and conjured up old fantasies of sexual adventure and orgy and came quietly in my pants while the ministers studied the history of the Protestant religion.

I wrote about every moment I had experienced with Benjamin, hoping that, perhaps if I tried hard enough, I would understand something. I tried to banish my mother to her grave as I had done once before, and to see Benjamin as a new person, precious, not to be burdened by all the intricacies of my too complicated history. After all, I would console myself, he is his father's child too.

I stopped reading about mythology, as I was supposed to be doing. Somehow I would pass my reading courses. The familiar activities of studying and writing papers joined my novel in the cloudy distance—all were lodged as if stuck in wet cement in some far-off dream. I withdrew into the details of caring for my baby in order to tolerate the immense passion which was growing within me, taking over what had once been my knowable soul. I knew I would never belong only to myself again.

I sat once a week and watched the trees, assigning my work to unimportant things of the past. I was a mother now.

One morning I threw my books all over the house, destroying them, tearing them. Then I threw James's books all over, hating him for still being involved in his work, for becoming a parent without having been pregnant or given birth, for holding the baby incorrectly and forgetting to put the dirty diapers out that morning, for making an appointment to go to a meeting when he knew perfectly well it was my day for the library, for suggesting each night as I lay down drowsily in front of the television that I study, for offering to drive me to school so I could nurse before and after my class, for not being as fascinated with me as a mother as he had been with me as a writer or student, for being exhausted from studying and giving the two-a.m. feeding, for not loving Benjamin as much as I did and for having become a parent and still having remained—in the eyes of the world and himself—a person too.

It was not fog, I knew, which clouded the train station that early morning when I waited for the 8:05 to New York, but my guilt made visible. I felt beyond pain or joy. Instead, what filled me was the sort of acceptance you feel one day after a loved one has died and, the first passionate period of mourning over at last, you say, Yes, he's dead. I must begin to live differently.

For two days every week I would be in New York attending classes. For two days and one night every week I would be away from Benjamin. I felt peaceful and expectant standing alone, frightened and exhilarated by this attempt to embrace once again my own life. But the deepest part of me leaned toward that moment on the following afternoon when I would return to my baby: I was changed forever.

I turned and waved good-by to James holding Benjamin in his arms. A bottle would have to suffice since I would be too far away to return, a baby-sitter would feed him and change him and perhaps kiss him. And wanting nothing more than to run back and hold him to me, I boarded the train.

Part Two

Mothers and Fathers

Remember, we don't love like the flowers, from a single

year only; when we love, arises in our arms

the sap from immemorial ages. O young girl,

this; that we loved within us, not one, one coming,

but the countless ones teeming; not a single child,

but the fathers who rest in our depths, like the ruins of mountains;

but the dry riverbed of foremothers; but the whole

silent landscape under the clear or

cloudy destiny: all this forestalled you, young woman.

RAINER MARIA RILKE, "The Third Elegy"

from Duino Elegies (English translation by C. F. MacIntyre)

6

It is nine o'clock in the morning and, since the day is cold and gleaming snow lies mountainously over everything, I sit on the bench alone. It is silent. Benjamin is silent in his carriage, wrapped snugly in several colorful blankets while the white glare of the snow forces his lids closed and the stinging air mutes his intensity; soon he will be asleep. The families behind all the large, floor-to-ceiling windows in the court are silent.

Then lights gleam behind the curtains. Husbands emerge, one by one, only their eyes showing out of the hats and scarves and coats which will see them through the long day, only their shining, hopeful eyes. Some of them wave to me as they trudge off down the stairs, heading toward the magnificent Gothic towers visible in the distance. The wives and children will be in the houses for another hour and a half. At ten-thirty, they will emerge: the children will play for a while in the snow; the court will ring with the screams and fights and whines and joy of little children; the mothers will peek at them periodically from the windows to make sure they are O.K. or perhaps they will come out for a bit of air themselves. They will shiver and I will shiver as we greet each other, and we will say something about the weather and something about the baby and nothing at all about our husbands, who will not be back to help with wet, cold, cranky children until it is dark, and nothing about ourselves. To each other and to the young children and to the absent men, we are mothers. I am Benjamin's mother and perhaps soon I will say good morning to Matthew's mother. I wait and I watch the windows, hoping no one will come out yet, hoping Benjamin and I can stand the cold for a while because the stinging on my cheeks and the tears in my eyes smooth out the jagged, unpleasant feelings which constantly threaten to rise to the surface of my mind in more comfortable surroundings. Somehow what is a welcomed and inspiring self-containment out here in the snow turns into a terrible loneliness the minute I go into my apartment. So, when I am too cold to sit on the bench any longer, I walk, feeling like a prison inmate let out for daily exercise, around and around the yard.

All of the apartments are identical and they ring a central court. In order to live in this housing complex, you must be a married student with children. Yet the famous architect who designed it all had obviously never lived with a child. There are too many corners around which a child may run suddenly, out of sight. There are ledges everywhere which tempt young children to climb but which are far too steep for safety. There is no way of leaving the court without going down a long flight of stairs or up a steep hill; thus, only with a great surging effort can a baby carriage be dragged onto the road. Most people use back packs, but my back is weak and after a few blocks I begin to feel a nagging pain around my waist; so each day I drag the baby carriage outside the prison walls. I imagine that the sturdy, midwestern girls, athletically slim and able to withstand great hardship, look at me and judge me to be a physically weak, slightly snobbish overly serious New Yorker, which is precisely what I defiantly am.

The walls of the apartments are thin so that even if your own child is quiet you can hear all the other children cry. You can also hear the married couples when they fight. I do not hear many of them, but the people above us, thankfully, scream at each other every night so that I feel better about my own, loud voice. The bedrooms are all back to back so you can also hear the sound of sex if it is above a whisper but we don't hear much of that either. James, having grown up in a similar kind of project and thus knowing the rules, often tells me to be quieter when we are making love, so I yell as loud as I can that I don't give a damn what they hear, and I put my mouth to the wall and announce that we are fucking now. Partly I do this because it is very funny to see James moan, Oh Lord, and pull the covers over his head in embarrassment, and partly because I have to shout very loud about everything these days because, except for the two days I am in New York, there is a real danger of losing faith in my existence. But one morning, emerging from my apartment into the court, I finally notice the distinctly odd looks which clearly know all about my anger and my passion and in general all of those things which, in the wonderful anonymity of a New York apartment, once comprised my "private life"; I decide to bow to James's greater wisdom about small communities and keep my voice down; during orgasm I learn to turn my head to the side so I can bite the pillow instead of loudly moaning and this turns out not to be as great a sacrifice as I had expected. It is harder to keep my voice down during fights with James, so during the day I am constantly wondering, when talking to some woman, how much she heard and what she knows and whether she is smirking at me behind her gracious smile.

Except for the few mothers who work at the university, we all wear unattractive pants and an old shirt. I often recall the feeling of looking beautiful or sophisticated which I experienced as a working woman in New York and I mourn a sense of stately, lost sexuality. In the warm autumn, when Benjamin was a newborn, I had remained in an unattractive housedress all day for several weeks.

Why should I get dressed? I had thought bitterly, when every three hours I have to get undressed to nurse? Why should I comb my hair, when soon it will be filled with spit-up, and lines of watery shit, dried and smelling, will run like little rivers down the front of my shirt, while on my shoulders, like the golden pads of old military glory, will be the white marks of a successful burp!?

And thinking I was punishing James and myself with an outrageous act of self-denial by walking around in a soiled bathrobe for days on end, I was shocked to discover several other young women doing the same thing, not only in their apartments, but out in the court, and without any sense of drama, but as if it were an ordinary thing for young, attractive women to dress in this manner. And their casual heedlessness of themselves made me run for the closet and, at least, a pair of clean dungarees and a tight-fitting sweater.

Years later, I would learn to see in those sloppy days a kind of freedom which was based on a strong, realistic understanding of what it means to be a parent of young children. For all of us, mothers and fathers, on our days at home with the children, would walk with the same physical heedlessness and, sharing the experience, we would know that it did not represent a lack of interest in sexuality or even in aesthetics, but a willingness to don the most practical uniform for the work at hand. And we would see beyond the soiled clothing and rumpled hair to the naked, open, still youthful bodies underneath the cloak of parenthood. Only certain nonparents would think we had abandoned all decent respect for sensuality. But then we would see their still competitive, obsessively cumulative concern with costume as a sign of their spiritual imprisonment while we, at least, had taken one step out of tyrannous materialism.

But in the early days of Benjamin's life, I would watch the women dressed in pants which had gone out of style years before and old wrinkled shirts belonging to their husbands, and I would be blinded by memories of blue velvet dresses and silver striped slippers and pink artificial flowers and, bouncing like a rubber ball between the two mother images assaulting me, I would run for a sequined belt to wear on my jeans or down to the store to buy a stylishly new sweater—because, at times, there were also, underneath the old loose clothing everyone wore, bodies which had grown fat from sexless nights and days which could be made exciting for a moment only by the taste of sweet cakes; and the premature lines on the faces of the women were the signs of a deep anger which, though meant for the men, was usually expressed toward the children, and, since that was often unfair, it was turned in, like a sword drawing bloody crevices, upon the self.

Just as I expected, at ten-thirty the women and their children opened their doors and, like so many jacks-in-the-box, popped out to join me. One woman came over to speak to me. There was some feeling of closeness between us as we had given birth to our sons only days apart, and we had spoken to each other many times before:

How is yours doing, oh how is yours doing, sleep through the night? Yes oh yes (she would say) and, No, not yet (I would have to report); and then, Cry much? No, very contented baby, it seems (she said proudly); and, Cries a lot, must not be contented (I barely whispered, feeling as though the Inquisition had discovered that I was a witch or the Welfare Department had found big red welts on my baby's back and would take him away from me and send him to a foster home).

She knew, I was certain, or should since the signs were there that I was an inadequate mother.

Why? I asked myself over and over. Why is my baby not contented? My friends, those who loved me, would tell me that my baby was intense and bright and all good things and that was why he rebelled so loudly against frustration. I knew one thing for sure. I loved him enough. Too much. Ah, maybe that was the trouble.

Was she lying? I wondered, this young, innocent, white and pink midwestern girl who had a good baby. Was her baby really as bad as mine, did he cry all night and nurse every hour instead of every four, and stay constipated for two or three days at a time, or was he really the way she declared him to be? I looked closely at her eyes, stared for so long that I made her uncomfortable, waited in ambush to spot a sign of hypocrisy in a line of her face, a twist of her mouth. But always she appeared to be even, serene, impenetrable. Once I listened at her baby's window for screams in the night. I heard none. I began to hate her and her baby.

When she came toward me in the snow that morning, smiling, I was free, at least, to be honest—despising her as I did and not caring about the impression I made. Here we were, my baby and I, sitting squarely on the outskirts of official normality, of conventional acceptability; they didn't talk about us in Dr. Spock—only in abnormal-psych books. I had forgotten how comfortable it was here on the outskirts, how, once abnormality had been accepted, freedom began to shove the ordinary sun away and fill up the sky with its own brilliant glow.

How's yours doing, sleep through the night, and aren't they wonderful? it began.

"No," I said, short and clipped. "No, he doesn't sleep through the night. No, it is not wonderful. Sometimes I wish I had never had a baby."

The way she looked at me I had to renege a bit, cowardly rebel that I was.

"Oh, I love him and everything."

She relaxed. Angry at my compromise, I attacked again.

"But I could kill him sometimes." I looked her in the eye. I ordered myself not to waver. I felt the girlwoman smile and took courage. I did not modify or placate. I kept silent. I felt her long look heat my face and wondered if she thought I really meant to kill him.

"It's cold," she said, vanquished by my gift for tolerating long, uncomfortable silences. And I smiled. Then she introduced a new topic.

"I have so much to do today," she gasped wearily, but the promise of efficiency could be heard in her voice.

What? I wondered and then asked out loud, brazen now, thinking of my own uneventful days, my long hours of staring, the deadening boredom which had established itself like dry heat right in the middle of my living room.

"It's Monday," she said as if in explanation. I must have looked quizzical, and like a schoolteacher who cannot quite believe her pupil's stupidity, she slowly elaborated.

"I have to wash so I can iron tomorrow. The house is a mess from the weekend. I have shopping to do and roasts to cook for the week and my husband's pants to get at the cleaner's."

"Can't he get his own damn pants?" I said, feeling virtuous because I had said *damn* instead of *motherfucking*. But in spite of that concession on my part, she was visibly hurt. And I had noticed before, when she was hurt or outraged, she responded with the secure and ritualistic comfort of litany.

" . . . Well, he's very busy, has a lot of pressure on him, stays up all night studying, I have to do my part, I don't mind, no I don't mind, no I don't mind, no I don't . . . "

"I would," I said. But then, thinking of all the hours of work this woman did, never receiving a salary, a day off, or a vacation, I began to feel sisterly, wanting to free her resentment by offering her mine, wishing she would recognize, even for a moment, my open anger as in some way kin to her own. But she did not. She was in no mood to capitulate. And no wonder. In a way, she had won. For surely she had noticed the determination and certainty drain from my eyes as I thought guiltily of James's tired face. I wished he had a wife like her, selfless and giving, I wished Benjamin had a mother like her, moderate and even. I wished I had a mother like her.

Benjamin began to cry, while her baby slept on for the third hour (she told me with confidence), and revealing an awesome ability to predict the future she assured me that she wouldn't have to nurse until twelve.

I picked up my baby and, wrapping him in his blankets, holding him to me away from the wind, I unbuttoned my coat and my sweater and shirt and, feeling the freezing wind against my wet skin, nursed him in the snow.

Well, that was a little too much for her and she left to wax the floors.

Soon I put Benjamin back in the carriage, on his stomach this time, and moved the pacifier into his mouth, hoping it would help him return to sleep. Then I took him back inside so we could thaw, wondering if I should risk waking him by taking off his snowsuit or risk his overheating by leaving it on.

For this sort of attention to detail had become the only pursuit which gave my day the possibility of order, providing me with the feeling that I still retained some measure of control over the course of my life.

Somehow I had made the right choice and, though he drenched his carriage sheet with sweat and woke up looking as if his hair had just been washed, he slept in his snowsuit and woolen hat for two blessed hours. Thus we were friends that afternoon.

We ate vanilla yogurt together and I saw the wonder which filled his eyes as he tasted it for the first time. Then we shared a jar of baby peaches, which I hadn't eaten since my sister and I had stored them in the kitchen cupboard for our midnight snacks when we were teenagers. Each dark night we would eat baby peaches together after we had finished our homework, when our father was asleep in his room.

Benjamin could smile now so we laughed together a lot as I fed him a spoonful and then one for me. There had been many times since his birth when I had called him by my sister's name. In the middle of the night when his cries dragged me mercilessly out of my precious dream, I would forget his name for a moment and scream—Pamela! Shut up! When I hated him I had called him Pamela. When I most loved him I had sometimes called him Pamela. As I fed him the peaches, I began to cry, overwhelmed for the thousandth time that day. I wondered if you could have a heart attack from the emotional intensity of being a mother. But I could see Benjamin getting upset so I stopped crying and we embraced. I lay down on the couch and put him on my stomach, and since he had recently learned to hold up his head, he looked at me. Then I sang him as many songs as I could think of, funny ones, sad ones, love songs and Negro spirituals and Yiddish lullabies. I stroked his face and, just when I wanted him to keep looking at me and cooing to the music, he fell asleep again. He stayed that way on my stomach for a long time. While I looked out that huge window at the snow.

Unable to keep my promise to hide my true feelings from the other mothers I met, I kept trying to find a coconspirator. With certain women, I would make one tentative risky statement and, seeing that either there was no hope or that their condemnation was more than I cared to endure, I would stop, retreating into silence or muted hostility. As soon as possible I would go off by myself.

With others, if they really annoyed me with their contentment, or if I was feeling strong anyway that day, I would push on, contradicting all the popular shibboleths about maternity, exaggerating even my sense of despair. My tolerance for myself, my acceptance of my apparently ubiq-

uitous oddness, the creeping return of familiar aspects of my personality, were all linked to one central fact: Benjamin had begun to sleep
through the night.

For three weeks we had clung to our determination that he could be
trained to sleep eight hours at a stretch. Listening to him cry out the
prescribed twenty minutes advised by Dr. Spock, clutching the pillow
into my sweaty palms, my head pounding with his screams, I tried to lie
still so as to drive out the image of the withdrawn, vanquished, perhaps
even autistic child I expected to find in the crib in the morning. When
the crying finally stopped and I was sure he was asleep, I would tiptoe
in, run my finger down his face, almost wake him with my concern.

When other babies cried, it seemed only like babies crying to me.
When Benjamin cried, it seemed like an accusation, a plea for help, a
desperate need, a moan of complete misery. I lay in bed imagining
babies snatched by Nazi soldiers from their mothers' arms. Sometimes,
not able to bear it, I would take him out of his crib, resigned to spending the hour between three and four A.M. walking him into slumber.
But as soon as I lifted him out of the bed, he would smile, dry-eyed and
evidently unharmed; he was obviously ready to play. I put him back in
the crib and for the next four nights James and I would time his crying
to the movement of the minute hand.

"It's been twenty minutes!" I would state, jumping out of bed with
the satisfaction of a prosecuting attorney who has defeated Dr. Spock at
last.

"It's only been eighteen!" James would respond, annoyed by my
endless exaggerations.

"Let's go get him now," I would say, wanting to hold him or hit him
but hating to lie there silently listening to him.

"Then he'll never learn and we'll never sleep," said James, who could
always be counted on to accurately interpret a miserable situation. But I
knew that if I held him tonight, I'd be holding him the next ten nights
too. One night Benjamin woke up five times. He was nine months old.
He was not sick and didn't appear to be teething. Two pediatricians had
told me that almost every child sleeps through the night by six months.

"But of course," I said sarcastically as I tossed in bed holding one,
two, three pillows over my ears, "not Benjamin."

Five times I gave in and fed him a bottle. The third, fourth and fifth
times, he pushed the bottle away, not hungry, no longer crying, in fact
smiling at me as we sat there together, staring at each other in the

middle of the night. His obvious contentment at having me instead of his crib beneath him so infuriated me that, calmly, I put him down in his crib and went back to bed, where to the music of his miserable cries, enjoying every second of his pain, I fell into a deep sleep. I do not know how long he cried. But after that he slept through the night.

Until he began teething again and we had to begin the process, wiser but just as weary, for the third time. By then I no longer cared about tribal women who sleep with their babies huddled to their breasts until the children are old enough to get up and walk away. I no longer cared about any abstract theories of infant development. I had learned one thing: without sleep I was a miserable, distraught, angry woman. I braved self-doubt, even the midnight assurance that I was a schizo-phrenogenic mother-figure; I clutched the pillow and endured, and finally I was rewarded. For once my will had been victorious over Benjamin's. He began to sleep through the night frequently enough for me to move toward a moderate restoration.

One day, sitting on the bench in the court off to myself, I was approached by a woman named Jean Rosenthal. She was the only other New York Jew living there and the only reason I had not spoken to her before was that she was rarely around. She looked rather wild, wore her skirts very short, her hair dyed flaming red, her eyes heavily made-up. Her son always seemed to be staying with a neighbor; it was the talk of the court that he was neglected, brilliant but neurotic, overly aggressive and unable to get along with his peers; it was also rumored that Jean was having an affair with her best friend's husband. I liked her.

I began my search for camaraderie by insulting the other women in the court. She not only agreed with my nasty remarks but went on to describe secrets and impart gossip which shocked and delighted me. She had lived in the court for two years, and she knew about illicit affairs, parties where husbands and wives switched, husbands who, when their civilized, intellectually stimulating, orderly days at the university were over, came home to beat their wives—actually physically beat them. I couldn't wait to tell James.

Then she told me about all the gossip which surrounded James and me. Either by some queer accident, or by the diabolical design of someone in the back room of the housing bureau, two other interracial couples had occupied our apartment before us. One had divorced. As for the second, the man had run off with another woman and the wife had been committed to the local psychiatric ward. People were waiting anxiously to see what would happen to us. There had also been great interest in inviting us to the switching parties—the women especially were desperately eager to weave their fingers in and out of James's erogenous zones until they grasped, once and for all, his large, black, powerful . . .

"Well, she didn't say all that," I would have to admit later to James's widening eyes, but the implication rang loudly behind her calmer description of the local orgies, I assured him confidently.

Having shared this moment of closeness, set pleasantly off from the others, I could certainly speak to Jean about motherhood. I began by referring to the women's movement which, by now, was spreading over the country, asking if she had ever been in a consciousness-raising group, telling her about my experiences. No, she hadn't, but she thought she would want to someday. Had she ever felt hatred for her child? Yes. Did she wonder if she should have been a mother? Yes. We decided to begin our own group for the mothers in the housing complex and recruit all of the oppressed women. We fashioned a leaflet:

TIRED OF BEING SOMEBODY'S MOTHER OR SOMEBODY'S WIFE? COME TO JEAN ROSENTHAL'S HOUSE ON MONDAY NIGHT. TALK ABOUT YOUR REAL FEELINGS. WOMEN'S GROUP FORMING.

We signed our names. Jean said she knew two other women who would definitely be interested and would sign their names to the announcement. One was Anna Magrino who lived at the apartment at the bottom of the hill. She had two children, stayed home full time and was quite miserable. The other was Karen Olin, who had become a mother when she was an unmarried eighteen-year-old girl. Her present husband was not the baby's father; she worked full time as a librarian. How had I missed these women? They never came out to the yard, Jean advised me. When she called them, they said, Yes, we could use their names. Once again I waited impatiently for the first meeting of a women's group; in this group, we would concentrate on motherhood, that would be our starting point; there would be no one to impress. I was like a rocket ship, waiting for the countdown, when I would be released, finally, into the broad freedom of the skies.

We all sat around Jean's large, disordered living room. There had been some attempt at straightening up the mess, I could see. But the room was very dirty. The floor showed black lines of heavily encrusted mud.

Crumbs from one of the endless snacks of a two-year-old littered the couch. Dirty dishes rose out of the sink and coffee cups, which were set out for us on a low table, had old stains on the inside and crusted remnants of previous meals on the outside. This was not the disorganized clutter of any normal house in which children live. I had grown used to the Fisher-Price people rolling around beneath my feet, the stray Tinker Toys hiding in every corner, the roll of toilet paper sitting oddly on the bookshelf because some little person had dragged it for the hundredth time out of the bathroom. This was different. Jean's house reflected an inability to control outside reality. She was living so intensely inside her head that she sometimes lost her connection to the outside world. She might sweep, but would always, maddeningly, miss half the dirt. She might decide to wash the dishes, but somehow they would never be clean, because by the time she had reached for the third dish she would be totally elsewhere. She might try to straighten, but would end up simply putting half-filled glasses which didn't belong on the floor on an end table where they didn't belong either. Beneath the inability to control this kind of dirt was an act of rebellion. But even the person herself did not know that secretly she was saying, Here is my anger; here is how much I despise you; here is how inadequate I am; here is the chaos inside me which masks those fearsome hatreds whose existence I cannot afford to notice. Here is the ugliness I see everywhere, in the world, in your face, in those secret, infested places where the roots of my actions are knotted into a thankfully unrecognizable mess.

I had been in many houses like this one. Mine had once been like it and sometimes threatened to become like it again. Yet, I was more comfortable here than in those other homes, where nothing was ever out of place, where surfaces were always bare and dust-free, where never more than two glasses and a spoon accumulated in the sink, where everything had its permanent place and where I felt that by sitting on a chair I was interrupting the décor of the room. For surely that room had not been intended for people to live in but rather had a life of its own. And that life gave far more sustenance to its owner than some unpredictable, uncontrollable human being.

I relaxed in Jean's living room which smelled slightly of many previous meals. I noticed Karen and Anna sitting near each other, waiting. Jean was getting coffee. There were three other women in the room.

One lived above me and it was a generally accepted fact that she was crazy. Another was one of the good mothers. I wondered what she would say. Next to her was someone I didn't know.

It was up to me to begin—I was the only one who had been in a group before. So, I began in the usual way.

"Perhaps we should go around in a circle, introduce ourselves, and say why we are here."

Jean went first. "I'm Martin's mother," she said and we all laughed, grateful that she had identified herself in this crucial way. Then, in soft tones, she described her discussion with me on the bench, how we decided to start the group, and all the while she kept on smiling. At the end, she said quietly and hesitantly, "I feel that I have certain problems in being a mother."

I thought of her little boy, speaking fluently at two, strong and rough with the other children. He was like Benjamin in some ways. Although barely one, Benjamin spoke many words, had been walking for two months, hit anyone who came near him. I was certain he was at the beginning of the long road to Alcatraz. However, Benjamin had never been found in the early morning sleeping in the drying machine in the laundry room which all the families shared, all curled up like a baby in the uterus, feeling the residual warmth of the drying cycles which were now finally still. It was the face of Jean's little boy that had looked out at the startled woman who found him there.

Knowing that we were all picturing that or some other similar incident, Jean smiled again and said, "Well, I'll let someone else speak now."

The woman I didn't know said, "I don't know why I'm here. I'll see what happens. It would be nice to get to know someone around here."

I could understand that, but the level of openness so far did not inspire me.

Patty, the crazy lady, was next. She contributed little about motherhood, but was honest in a way that would continue to shock us in the coming weeks. She spoke straight from an embarrassingly unhidden spot way inside herself. She had no comfortable, conventional masks to use in ordinary light company. When she tried the masks most other people used, they were always tearing, exposing raw skin.

"I've been in a mental hospital twice," she would say to us later, casually; "many people think I'm crazy." Then she would smile sarcastically, her eyes laughing, and would continue in a high-pitched, mocking voice, "But my husband, now, he's a real chauvinist pig." And she would wait for the applause of acceptance.

On that first night she said, "I saw your four names on the announcement and I figured if you four were organizing it, it would be interesting. I have noticed all of you, sitting around, and have wished I were like you."

I twitched uncomfortably, seeing that I and the others had come to occupy some sort of ready-made niche in her head and, since she didn't know me at all, that niche might very well be furnished with all sorts of associations which I would undoubtedly find cumbersome and even burdensome to live with. But I was glad Patty was in the group. Crazy people could be counted on to break through a more impenetrable sort of artificiality, the sort which was practiced by those who were "well-adjusted," who fitted the world in which they lived like a piece of a child's simple five-piece puzzle. Crazy people could be counted on to say out loud what others were thinking.

It was Karen's turn. She immediately reinforced her one, shining, enviable difference.

"I work full time," she said, tossing her beautiful blond hair just slightly. "And my son is already six." We all shifted position, bit a lip or smiled jealously. Seeing she had been successful, she softened. "But I'm sure I feel many of the things you do, and I might have another child soon." Her light-blue pants suit gleamed dramatically from the background of our dungarees. Her eyes were well made-up. I could see her body move beneath her pretty clothes, I could picture her breasts, which seemed very round for someone who had given birth. She was thin and vain.

Karen's obvious pride in her body attracted me. Women who in some way clearly love themselves are often capable of great love for other women. And I experienced a pleasant feeling of satisfaction as she spoke. I was glad she was in the group, excited by the hope of being her friend.

Next the good mother spoke. She talked about how much she loved her baby, and paused to see if anyone would condemn her. She said that her husband would never help on an equal basis with either the housework or the child, and that was the way she wanted it.

Jean asked why she had come. She answered that she just wanted to see what it was about. Collecting all of my waning sense of sisterhood, I tried to ignore the bloodthirsty smile on my girlwoman's face.

It was Anna's turn. "Well, what can I say," she began, and looking at Jean, whom she obviously knew well, for support, she let out a loud, throaty guffaw. But it wasn't a crazy laugh—like those hilarious giggles and inappropriate explosions that come suddenly out of an otherwise serious face, letting you know immediately that the person is lost inside, that the part of the person laughing is in no contact at all with the part that is not. No, Anna's laugh was total. She was laughing at herself, at what she was about to say. She seemed to be laughing at all of us. But Anna was one unified person inside, and that person was standing slightly apart, commenting on the absurdity of her life, and daring anyone else to judge her.

She looked around at us again, seemed to decide something, and began slowly.

"Being a mother is a terrible thing. It ruins your relationship with your husband. It ruins your life. You can't leave them because you love them and when you're with them you hate them. I used to be a damn good nurse. Very competent. I've nursed people all over the world. I ran an entire ward in Boston. Now I'm a mother, and that means I'm nothing. I don't know. There are good things too. But really," she was speaking loudly, clearly now and with a great seriousness, "I feel as if I am on the verge of cracking up."

And she laughed out loud again. We were all quiet. Then, uncomfortable, reaching back for the security of our circle of talk, the other women looked at me. And like a child in school who sounds as if she is afraid to speak but who is merely speaking the simplest truth, I said, "I agree with everything Anna just said."

And with that statement something fell off, crumbled, disintegrated within me—the wall which had kept me alone, the prison cell, the solitary confinement, and the terrible possibility that even in this universally feminine experience, I would still be, at least to myself, horribly odd—all these were cracked by the familiarity of Anna's words and began to fall away.

From the beginning of my pregnancy and as far back as I could remember, I had sought relatedness. But as a child they had called me strange and special and then better or even best, and Pamela had hated me for it. Later I had been isolated by the definitions of maternity which seemed inevitably to stop short right outside the reality of my experience. The modern books about controlled, graceful pain, the obstetrician's condescending commandments, the glaring spotlight on the

lonely stage of the delivery table where I lay so passionately alive surrounded by ghosts and skeletons in death masks, the horrible child-care
books full of threats and promises of torture, the enslaved faces of so
many women whom I wanted to love, but whose spirits had been
beaten into indistinguishable masses of illusion—all had resulted in
convincing me that I was, still, after all of this, alone. And I lived in an
exile whose inner turmoil and outer dullness threatened to shatter my
sanity and keep me wandering over barren deserts, beating all the while
on the slammed doors of kinship.

Now here was Anna. I am a living woman, I heard her saying. And as
she spoke my thoughts out loud, the loneliness began to fall away. I
loved her immediately.

For the next several months, Anna and I practically lived together. She
spoke about things which I had only dared write in my record books.
Yet she was even more crippled than I by the demands of motherhood.
She had given birth to two children in the space of one year. She had not
even considered the possibility of leaving them with baby-sitters. And
still bound to elements of her Catholic upbringing, she was unable to
use birth control so that each month she waited, sweating and shiver-
ing, for her period. She had already had one miscarriage in the year
since her younger child had been born. She needed something I could
give her: I argued her out of her Christian intimidation and accompanied her to a doctor who fitted her for a coil. In return, I took her total
inability to hide her feelings, as ugly and outrageous as they might be.

Trusting each other, seeing how much we were alike, we began
taking care of each other's children. And leaving them with each other,
we were able to concentrate on something besides the moment of
reunion.

I studied my mythology books with the sort of attention I had not
been able to call forth in over a year. Anna attended courses which
interested her, walked alone through town, for the first time in two and
one-half years, alone. While we watched the children together, or at
night after they had gone to sleep, we talked about them.

"I love them and everything, but I hate them," she would say.

"I would die for him," I emphasized. "All those movies about
mothers running in front of trucks and bullets to save their children are
true. I would much prefer to die than lose him. I guess that's love"—I
winced and we both laughed—"but he has destroyed my life and I live
only to find a way of getting it back again." I finished slowly, for without

the second part of the sentence, the first part was a treacherous lie—a lie we had sworn to be done with.

"I can't wait until tomorrow, when it is your day to keep the children," she would say, "but I dread leaving them in the morning." We learned always to expect sentences to have two parts, the second seeming to contradict the first, the unity lying only in our growing ability to tolerate ambivalence—for that is what motherly love is like.

At the weekly meetings with Jean, Karen and Patty, we felt our fragile beliefs become entrenched into indestructible knowledge as the three other women said, Yes, yes, me too, and told their own stories of motherhood.

The good mother and the woman who was looking for friendship had not returned. They were angry or frightened, or perhaps only bored, too happy with their children to tolerate all of our complaints, or too miserable and weakened to risk the terror of listening. I no longer cared which.

Instead, I listened to Karen tell about the years when her son was a baby while she was a little girl.

"Now that he is six," she said once, "the hard times are over. He lets himself in the house after school and calls me at work to tell me about his day. Sometimes while I am taking a bath, he comes in and soaps my back and talks about how my breasts are beautiful." She blushed. But there being no expert in the room to draw conclusions about this sort of behavior, we, mere mothers ourselves, were respectfully silent.

Annoyed at times and impatient, we nevertheless listened to Patty weave her webs of self-hatred and anger in the middle of the room— each week a new web, each week a new tale of bizarre cruelty grabbed out of the burning cold days of her childhood in Vermont. And always at the end of the story, in the middle of her web, entangled in the net of her creation and quite beyond recognition, sat her husband. He was a successful student in graduate school, and had affairs with many women who were more beautiful and sane than Patty. None of us could understand what had brought these two together. What held them together was their son. Crippled at birth, unable to play as fast or as hard as the other children, forced, as a result of some chemical imbalance, to eat raw vegetables as an afternoon treat instead of sweets of any sort—he would limp out to the playground in the court and speak to the others as they ran past, or stand at the bottom of the stairs to the slide and joke with those waiting their turn to climb up and slide down. With the babies, like Benjamin, he was gentle—not only patient but interested. And it was not long before the other children were throwing their candy away half-finished and begging for one of his crisp string beans. He seemed unembarrassed when, every afternoon, his mother would run wildly out of the house, flailing a spoon in the air with one hand and his medicine bottle with the other, yelling that it was past time for his dose. Calmly he would walk over, say, "It's O.K., Mother," and drink the gooey pink liquid without a complaint: he knew he needed it to live.

I often thought that Patty had poured all the precious few drops of love which she had into that boy. And I even saw his father, known to me only through the evil actions which had been carefully described by Patty, walking with him every day, holding his hand confidently, kissing him every so often in between their sedentary, quiet games.

Soon it became clear to all of us that many of the families in the court were changing, as the anger released by the women's movement moved behind the big floor-to-ceiling windows, seeped under the thin doors.

Men began to appear in the playground with their children, even during the week. The good mothers, if not visibly changing their own lives, had, at least, to take our ravings more seriously. Divorce tore throughout the court.

One night a man came to visit James and me. He was a student at the law school, a passing acquaintance. Two years before his wife had been very active in the Law Wives Association. They had two blond children—a year and a half apart because of the advantages of siblings' being close in age. I had imagined his wife to be a "good mother." Yet on several occasions we had spoken, if superficially at least honestly, about some of the difficulties of motherhood: she was tired of doing her husband's shirts and thought she would start sending them to the laundry; she was worried about her daughter who seemed to cry so easily and never fought to defend herself against the more aggressive children.

Now the good mother was gone. She and the husband of a neighbor had left their families and gone off to live in town together. There had been many such liaisons in the court. The rumor about Jean and her friend's husband was true. And Jean's husband had, for a long time now, been sleeping with another woman whose own husband had gone off to practice medicine in South America with a fellow student's wife. At first it seemed unbelievable to me. Each day we would hear of another family exchange. And it would never be a neat swap, but always two people would be left behind, uninterested in each other, burdened with the total care of the children, usually without money and always dazed, never having imagined that the stakes of party switching mixed with self-denial would be so high.

Now this frightened, flabbergasted man from somewhere in Oregon sat in our living room and wept. He hardly knew us. Perhaps for that reason he chose to tell us that for a year Carol had not enjoyed sex with him, had finally stopped pretending. He wondered what he would do with his children.

My father's confused face looking down at us after our mother died swam in my head. The young student held out his hands desperately. He didn't know how to change a diaper; he didn't know what they ate for breakfast or lunch; he had no idea who needed inoculations or check-ups; how could he go to school and keep getting up in the night to hold his son who was continually crying for his mother?

He must have learned, though. I saw him every day after his classes, playing with the children for a while in the court. Then he would go in the house and by six would emerge looking tired and call them in to dinner. The little one seemed dry often enough, so I supposed he learned to change diapers. I noticed that he also learned to hang wash on the line and after a week there were no shirts in the bundle of clothes; he must have taken them to the laundry. His eyes shone a bit less, but his face grew handsome to me, older, more tolerant. One evening I went to his apartment to see how he was doing. We had not spoken since the strange night right after she left him when he had wept in our living room.

His apartment looked different. It was messier than Carol had kept it. The children's paintings hung on the living-room walls next to the well-framed prints. Toys were everywhere. He had just put the children to bed and he sat down, tired.

"Carol might be coming back," he told me. "She's considering trying again, starting over. We'll go to Alaska, somewhere far away, and do things differently."

"The children . . . " I responded, understanding her choice.

"Yes, the children, and a little bit me," he said, smiling.

In the afternoon, from then on, twice or three times a week, Carol would come into the court, pick up the children and drive away with them. They would run to her yelling, "Mommy, Mommy," and she would hug them, hiding her face from them while she cried. Then she would walk quickly past her former friends, not able to stand having either to act out or refuse to act out old expectations. She would get into her car, put the children in the back and drive away.

Anna and I would watch quietly as we stood in the court, arms folded, looking toward the end of the day. We would watch as Carol hugged her children, not having seen them for a week.

When I was seven, and my mother had just died, I was a monitor at school. My post was an outside door. I stood there every morning and watched the mothers bring their children to school. There was one woman whose hair was dark like my mother's and who was small as she had been. I would begin watching her as she appeared at the corner, walking her little boy down the block. I would watch her all the way to my door. When she bent down to kiss him good-by, I watched especially closely trying to feel on my face the feelings he felt on his. After the little boy went into school his mother would look at me uncomfortably, smile slightly, and turn away. I would watch her until she disappeared.

I tried to be very kind to Carol's children on the days when she didn't come for them. I was likely to hold Benjamin more frequently, to be more patient with his complaints and cries.

Benjamin and Anna's two boys sat in the bathtub together and played. I was washing them tonight while Anna's husband cooked. I liked washing them this way, all together, seeing their little bodies shine with the soap and then pouring water over them, first one pair of feet, then another, then another. One face, then yours, now yours. When they splashed me too much I yelled at them and threatened to take them out, and for a moment they would stop. When they did it again, since dinner was ready anyway, I would drag Billy out, feigning punishment so they would know I meant business, and since he was the most compliant of the three at that age, he didn't protest much. That was why I chose him. I hated to have Benjamin and David shriek at me. Wrapping the last child in a big towel and perching them all on a high table from which they dared not move, I dressed one and let him run into the kitchen, then two, then three. And with someone else taking care of dinner, I was free to slowly pick up the wet towels, put the soiled clothes in the bin, straighten the room and mop the bathroom—all peacefully, pleasantly, thinking to myself about my day, making pleasant order out of the pleasant mess of children, watching my hands which were losing their childish softness and, unmistakably, especially around the knuckles, were beginning to look like a mother's hands to me.

I heard James come in the door to Anna's apartment, and with him there to help with dinner now, Anna came in to help me. We talked in that way which had come to mean so much to me.

"I was worried when Benjamin bit that kid today—what's wrong with him?"

"Nothing, you idiot—he's fine. He's just very active, active and bright."

"So are your kids, but they don't fight as much."

"Well, my kids are shy, too intimidated."

"No, they're beautiful, fine."

Our words, like the words of the pink and white good mother in the snow, were beginning to have their own litany, but now it was a chant which strengthened, which I believed in at the bottom of my heart.

He is fine and beautiful and has his faults, there is such a thing as inherited temperament, and you are a good mother too—it went—a good mother too.

By the time James and Benjamin and I went back to our apartment, Benjamin was tired and dressed for sleep. In the morning, since now Anna's husband and James each took one day with the children along with us, I would go off for the third day that week to the library, where I would study mythology and still have time to write in my record book. Tomorrow it would be our turn to have Anna's family for dinner, and I thought I would bake chicken and made a big salad because that was what Anna liked best.

Spring was warm that year and James and I walked slowly to our apartment, taking turns hugging Benjamin, laughing as he kissed us, holding our necks with his small arms.

When my sister was very little, her knuckles didn't pop out like mine, but went in, surrounded by the hilly plumpness of baby skin.

When I was very little my mother sang me many songs at night as I fell asleep, songs which I still remembered and sang to Benjamin.

When I was a child my mother worked. If it were not that most of my friends' mothers stayed home and cooked and cleaned and picked them up at school, I wouldn't have cared. Because at night we would take a bath together. And whenever I got something in my eye, she would take it out knowledgeably and gently.

That night I wished that the next day were not mine to study but mine, instead, to stay with the children, so that I could relax in the morning, spend all day out in the grass feeling the sun and know that at five when the others came home to take over the evening responsibilities, I could rest, watching the children but not having to take care of them.

Then my mother's face filled my head, pushing everything else away. And it was with her hand that I patted Benjamin's back until he was asleep and it was with her voice that I sang to him.

7

Young men and women in long black robes pass before me. Their eyes are shining, burning into a dry spot in my head which, like a beach before a storm, is full of heated winds and delicate grasses which are uprooted by the wind and blown away. I watch as each new tuft of gentle grass flies down the beach, watch until the sandy world is bare and the water begins to rise. Then I stand up and walk.

I follow the men and women in long black robes who are all animated and smiling. James is among them. Like the rest, he is smiling. I feel my mouth curve upward, forcing my cheeks to puff up until I am smiling too, while my eyes, windows for me as I sit on the dark and windy beach, stay still. The backs of their heads are bouncing and turning—oh, one is waving to me—they must be talking, probably planning, comparing dreams.

This far James has come—all the way to this from the colored side of town. And there are twelve others like him. They give each other special looks as they walk to the front-row seats. Proud. Some of them are my friends. Several despise me for my color and my appropriation of a Black man. But all of them, from the pain of fighting for so long, are, for the moment, beautiful to me.

Sitting in the back, I come off the windy beach and stand up to look for James, telling his parents, "There he is, there he is"—watching them lean back making themselves comfortable, feeling they belong amidst all this Gothic wonder, proud not only of James, their boy, but of all those grown-up Black children, in front, sitting together.

Marie and I take turns holding Benjamin down. "Shhh," we keep saying. "There's Daddy."

"Daddy! Daddy!" he yells.

"Shhh," we say.

One by one they rise and walk to the little stage. "Thank you," each one says to the old man and, "Congratulations," he answers.

James's head moves. "There he is," I whisper to his brother and snap goes the camera. I can see when he turns to smile at us that he is embarrassed by the emotions which engulf him, and by my thoughts which, at such moments, he can read, and by the memories of the angry changes we have come through in these years of pregnancy and parenthood. How different we are, he thinks, catching Benjamin's eye, and, "Hi, honey!" he yells to him.

So now I have to hold Benjamin with an iron grip to keep him on my lap and talk about the wind when he asks me, "Why are you crying, Mommy?"

Yes, I answer James, How different we are. We have come this far now, to look at each other like this over Benjamin's curly head, and still, there is that line between your chin and your shoulder, I can just make it out under the long black gown, still beautiful.

Once more he looks at me, and down, shy almost or ashamed: the things we have said to each other, the terrible words, the names you have called me—accusations come to me from him, but softly.

I answer with a smile, apologetic but resigned. For I am thinking, You have fallen from your pedestal, Superman. I know what your quiet strength is now. It is a brick wall which magically arises behind your eyes when you want to banish me from your world. I, in return, have learned to live more and more parts of my life without you.

Remember? This was our first fight about Benjamin: he had cried and cried all day. You came home from school excited about something, and ignoring my pain-filled face, you pretended you were speaking to the woman you once knew.

Oh, wait till you hear about this and that, you began. Your excitement grew and your voice went faster and faster. Benjamin, draped over my shoulder, whined on and on, filling my head with screams. You know my face and its signs of trouble inside, yet you denied me.

This and that and my school and my ideas and very interesting concept, you said to me. Knowing that it was an idea in which I had once been interested, you were trying to make a bridge to this unpleasant woman who had replaced your once interesting and receptive wife.

"Don't you realize I don't hear anything you say!" I screamed. "Don't you hear him whining?"

Long lines of wives making their husbands comfortable when they come home from work, asking about the pressures of the day, a drink perhaps? or a moment to rest? presenting the house just cleaned and the hair just combed, long lines of them marched back and forth in me.

"I just walked in, I was just trying to tell you about my day," you said, knowing you had the historical advantage; but my day went unnoticed. Because you knew what it had been like and, not liking to be depressed, you didn't want to hear. So you placated and covered over.

Seeming magnanimous, you said you would take the baby and I should go in and lie down. But not ten minutes later he was screaming again. I waited. He kept on screaming. When I walked out to see, you were on the couch reading your paper and he was in the carriage screaming. I looked at you furiously and you exploded, "Look, I can't stop him, just let him scream. Fuck him."

I checked his diaper, which was wet through to his clothes. Changing him roughly, angrier than Benjamin, I began to call you the awful names I had never called you before, but then, I had never been this far into the realms of outraged fury. "You motherfucking asshole, you goddamn pig," and all the rest. Names you never called me, which I swore never to call you again. And I tried to tell you what it was like for me.

"Why is he mostly my baby? Do you think I know what I'm doing?"

"Well, I don't know, maybe there is something to maternal instinct."

"No (sarcastically), there is no maternal instinct, I just keep trying until he quiets down, that's all. I feel committed to him. You try for five minutes and say, Fuck him, and read your goddamn paper."

"Look," you said (and would many more times to me), "I don't blame you for hating it. Why don't we get a sitter for him?" you said, forgetting about my dead mother and dismissing what Benjamin might need as well as the love I felt. Your rule was, if I felt love, I wasn't allowed to express hate.

We talked a lot about what it was like to be a mother. I made you learn with my screaming and my demands and my precious selfishness. "Why should I go down the drain alone?" I asked. "It's your baby too."

There was something else. We found out about your patience and your inner calm. It was Benjamin who discovered them. Oh, I said one night as you quieted him into slumber, "Look at your maternal instinct."

You, to my astonishment and joy, were quite proud. "Daddy's little man," you began to sing as you rocked him.

We made a chart of duties. Monday, Tuesday, Wednesday I got up in the morning. Thursday, Friday, Saturday and Sunday you did. You got the extra day because I did so much more than you.

Still, many mornings on your turn, you would forget to close my door, or you would let him cry while you read the newspaper.

"Goddamn you," I would stalk into the living room.

"Goddamn it," you would answer. "What the fuck do you want me to do? So I forgot to close the door."

There were many times like that.

In the dark night, after I had held you on top of me, felt you come in me, watched your beautiful eyes closed, your mouth opened by the pressure of your passion, I would clutch your hand and we would wonder if this would drive us apart, as if there were something bigger than either of us which might be victorious over love.

But love had changed. And if we had not seen that just in time, we would have gone our own ways. And one more thing: I simply couldn't live that motherwife life—you saw that; I was desperate. I needed you to help me. *Help me*, not just support me; not on Sundays and special occasions, *Help me*, all the days and the nights, *raise our child with me*. I had this going for me: you liked me better the old way. You had a mother who loved you and you didn't need another one. You had a mother who didn't hide the truth from you and your brothers with soft tones and pedagogical manipulation in place of anger: "A woman's life ain't easy," she said. You saw her sweat all day and fall asleep early on the couch. You were attracted to my strength and helped me hang on.

For a long time, I had to remind you of everything: the diapers go out on Tuesday, the rubber pants are in the left-hand drawer, he needs an undershirt at night, the number of the pediatrician is 799-8090, don't forget we need vitamins and cereal, if you don't wake him from his nap by two, he won't go to sleep until ten, had a bath last night, needs a measles shot, alcohol on the unhealed navel and Vaseline on the circumcision, medicine three times a day—now it's time, and here's a good way to rock him.

I was the boss. But it was half the responsibility I needed to be rid of. Frightened that I couldn't trust you, I had to let you take it on yourself. It took almost two years, but that finally is what engaged your interest. Once I had to ask *you* if he needed a polio booster, and I was happy for days.

But there was one difference; you kept on going to school all day, so that here we are now watching you in your long black robe, walking proudly. And knowing all you have come through, I am more proud than anyone. Proud that Benjamin wants to be held by his daddy as much as his mommy, that either of us will do for him: that much work you have put into his growth—he loves you like a mother.

I took two courses a term. I am nowhere near finished with my degree. I couldn't leave Benjamin as often as you did, just couldn't manage to do it when he was so little. What do I have to show for these years, James? I have a baby. No one cares about that.

So I go back to my sandy beach where the water is rising, where no ritual or long black costume marks the changes I have known, where no audience acknowledges my struggle with their tears and clapping hands, where, with every low tide, another storm threatens.

8

For as long as she is visible, I watch Anna from the back window of the car. When I can no longer see her, I feel her crying. We will not live far from each other, an hour or so on the train. But the children will not bathe together every night and meet yelling with joy every morning. She will not take care of Benjamin once a week, nor will her husband. Nor will James, because he has a job. Well, I will have to find something, I think nervously as we ride down the Merritt Parkway. Leaves arch over us as we move down the road. I have grown used to leaves; perhaps I will miss the colorful boundaries they lend to my moods. Maybe when we find an apartment our block will have a tree on it.

The interminably unfinished double-decker bridges of the Cross Bronx Expressway signal my city is not far away. And almost every exit on the West Side Highway marks some period of my childhood.

"That's where we got off to go to the country when I was a little girl," I tell Benjamin. He looks at me closely, trying to see the little girl in his mommy's face.

"There is the place where we turn off to go to Aunt May's," I tell him.

And finally we come to the exit which has always been the end of the West Side Highway for me, where year after year, coming back from everywhere, I would think, Now we're home.

The light, simple stretches of gray and cobblestone, the Hudson docks where we watched for the *Queen Mary*, end abruptly. We bump down the exit and are in the streets going east.

Here is where they would wake me when I was a child and I would have to begin crawling out of the warm car blanket and get my shoes on, wondering how the trip had gone so fast when, on the way there, it had seemed neverending. "We're home already?" I would whine.

The cobblestoned street we lived on is asphalt now. And the iceman with his old horse and wagon doesn't come any more. Across the street, in place of the little brownstones which, one year, they painted yellow, pink and blue, is a white highrise called the Greenwich Arms. But the women's prison is still there, and as I get out of the car I hear them calling as they always have, "Here I am!!! Up here, motherfucker. Where is Millie, didn't she come?"

No matter how often I looked up, I never saw a face in one of those windows.

For three months we lived in my father's house, down the block from the women's prison. For the third time in the two years since I had become a mother, I decided that my baby needed me to be with him all the time. Perhaps it was living in my old home like this with my father; perhaps it was that I was irreversibly divided, made up of two opposite sorts of women and periodically each held sway over the other; perhaps it was that I knew no one I trusted to leave him with—perhaps it was the proximity of the women's prison. But whatever it was, I was not attending school that summer.

"This will be a good time to stay home with Benjamin," I told myself, thinking, Two months is not a very long time, forgetting what it is like to be always watching the clock, wondering how you will fill up the day.

I would plan my day as I had when, during my college years, I had worked as a file clerk: If I wait until two to go to lunch, then by the time I return there will be only two hours to go.

Now I planned my days again, my motive always to beat the clock.

"Benjamin, it's you and me," I would say each morning after James and my father left for work, trying to be clever, swearing to be patient, praying that today, one more day, I would be a good mother.

To begin with, I would try to remember the movements mothers were supposed to make, the things they did which brought security and order to things.

I walked from room to room making the beds, picking up stray toys, and then opening shades, clearing off glasses from the night before, sweeping the floor.

Two glasses I have missed sail through the air, crashing onto the floor while Benjamin, thinking he has made a great joke, stands proudly going rmmmm! rmmmmm! like an airplane.

I sweep, cursing. "Just for one minute I would like to see this room without a mess in it, Benjamin!"

"I want to go to the park! I want to go out!"

"Yes. But only if you stop throwing things around and let me have my coffee."

"Mommy's coffee. Hot. Hot," he whispers ominously. "No. No," he says firmly as he tries to grab my coffee. But I'm too fast for him and he misses. Realizing I'm still in control, practicing being a good mother, I laugh.

The days all roll around me in a circle, each one, though differing in detail, an exact replica of the one before.

I am holding Benjamin so he can wave good-by out the window to his daddy and grandpa.

I am writing a list of things for dinner.

I am holding Benjamin down with all my strength so I can put his clothes on without chasing him all over the house, and then listening to him scream outraged because he has to wait in his crib while I get dressed. I fix a bottle while he screams, "Bottie! Bottie!" looking as if he has just crossed the Sahara desert and I am making him crawl the very last foot to the oasis. I dump him and his bottie in the carriage, trying to remember to throw in my keys, some money, pail and shovel in case we go to the park, extra Pampers . . .

One morning after attending to all the things which needed attention and taking two aspirins, I walked out into the summer heat, pushing the worn and squeaky carriage before me and thinking, You are a selfish woman. Every job has unpleasant details. Every job has boring aspects.

Then, since it was only nine, I got my father's shirts at the laundry, my pants at the cleaner's and a paper.

At the corner I thought, But every other job is paid for.

Then, since it was only nine-thirty, I shopped for dinner. I wondered if the supermarket clerks could see the fatigue on my face, the anger in my eyes. No, they seemed miraculously to think I was an ordinary mother. But ordinary mothers, I was certain, did not move through their days hoping to remain in control for just one more hour, sitting to the side of themselves, always judging, laughing, humiliating the woman who lives through the day as best she can, trying to ignore the sun blaze of consciousness which transforms the ordinary world into a caricature.

Look at that ordinary housewife and mother, the mocking woman would taunt, her husband is at work. She is the little woman.

Walking down the cereal aisle, I saw some children accompanied by housekeepers and maids. Envying their mothers off at work, I touched Benjamin's soft, fat fingers wishing I were one sort of woman or another.

In the stores the men behind the counters called me "dear." One called me "little miss" but I jumped away before he could paste a pink bow on my forehead.

Or they flashed sex at me through vulgar mouths, making sounds of disgusting passion. One flashed his penis at me. I gagged all the way home.

Just as I was ruminating upon the connections between pink bows and unrequested penises, a woman yelled out of one of the highest windows of the prison, "Come in here with me, you little whore."

I looked up, uncertain if she were speaking to me. And then she said, clarifying my confusion, "Yes, you, baby, come to Mama."

I waited impatiently for the night when, away from all of them, I could go to sleep.

The days keep rolling around me, but the nights—the nights are always different.

One night I abandon my child. When I realize that I have left him alone, I run back to the elevator to get him. Instead of the old, gray metal, the elevator is carved wood, beautiful designs inlaid with gold. Suddenly I notice that it is broken and will not stop. It bursts out of the side of the building and lands on the ground, leaving me as far from Benjamin as ever. And then I become James. I (James) am filled with desperation, worried about Benjamin who, someone warns me, may be dead. I run up the stairs. On the way I discover I am in a museum which is filled with magnificent sculpture, all of which has been left to me in a will. What will I do with it? I wonder. Well, I will have to display it someday. Just as I reach the door to the apartment, the house disappears and I am outside again.

One morning it rained, so I did not go to the cleaner's and laundry and supermarket. When the rain stopped it was ten-thirty so I went straight to the park. In the playground, I realized I had remembered the pail but forgotten the shovel. "I want a shovel," Benjamin yelled, eyeing one in the nearest child's hand. I felt desperate, frightened he would betray me by fighting, hitting some gentle, obedient, normal child. He grabbed the shovel and when she tried to get it back, he socked her in the arm.

"No no. No, no. We don't hit," said the little girl's mother, wagging her finger.

"Goddamn it, Benjamin," I said and smacked him on his arm, wishing I had acted like the other woman. I took Benjamin off to the side, put my hand gently on his shoulder, appearing maternal, and whispered, "If you hit one more fucking child I will smack you so hard you will be black and blue." He shook his head up and down, scared of me, and promised to be good. Then, avoiding the eyes of the other women, I got him interested in the water pouring out of the drinking fountain into a little canal in the sand. I sat back on the bench, hoping that I would be allowed to stay there for perhaps fifteen minutes, and stared out into the world, always keeping Benjamin in the corner of my vision; frightened that I could frighten him so easily, I wondered why, since I spoke to him the way I often did, he still seemed to love me so much. And there was no doubting it. In the few blessed moments of objectivity I could grasp out of my interminably interior days, he seemed like a normal enough child. Maybe the other mothers did the same thing to their children, but in private. Or perhaps you didn't hurt a child as much as people believed by exploding, very often, in anger. No—surely it was more individual than that. It was more likely that, being my son, Benjamin instinctively understood me.

The next time he hit the little girl, I grabbed him and threw him in his carriage. When I got him in the house, I yelled at him for almost half an hour, talking to him as if he were twenty, preaching a sermon and screaming about morality and righteousness. He kept on shaking his head, looking at me with unmistakable apology in his eyes, finally breaking through my rage so I could see the child before me. What am I doing to this baby? I thought, and held him, forgiving him for not being the perfect creation of a magnificent mother.

"You were mean to the little girl," I whispered, "just as I'm mean sometimes. We'll both try to stop."

The accusing eyes of the other mothers who had somehow managed to remain proud sovereigns over their bitterness, at least in public, faded from my memory for a while. And around and around the days went.

One morning, reluctant to face the loneliness which waited for me on the park bench, I walked west. The parallel streets and avenues disappeared as, relieved, I reached the more disorderly streets of the Village. I came to the antique shops. Window after window filled with beautiful old chests, intricately carved rockers, painted china lamps. The crystal prisms reflecting the colors of summer turned the city into something wonderful, as it had once been. Away from the park and all the definitions lurking behind the trees, I didn't mind so much being Benjamin's mother. I showed him the blue, green and pink stars shining in the crystal. We ate Italian pastry together.

But in the afternoon, remembering Dr. Spock's heavily printed, underlined commandment that toddlers spend part of EVERY day with other children, I went back to my bench. We met a junkie that afternoon who grabbed Benjamin's pail so he could use it as a drinking cup. Then he threw it on the ground.

Often, as I walked through the streets in the morning, I would clutch the carriage handle tightly, frightened by the violence of my thoughts.

"Mmmmmm. You have a pretty mommy," said the vegetable man caressing the broccoli, looking from me to Benjamin and back again. I lopped off his penis with an ax which I whipped out of the carriage bag where it had waited for an occasion just such as this one.

Immeasurably weary of the recurring boredom I always met inside my head, immeasurably weary, I had begun to decorate my fantasies with the weapons of death. One! Two! Three! Four! went the penises onto the ground. And sometimes, decimated by the bombs I threw, whole blocks would cave in.

At night, I took a bath with Benjamin. The moment he was naked, I forgot all my anger. I sat in the warm water and watched him play. I covered him with bubbles, he put one on my nose.

"Oh, Mommy," he said, full of love, slippery in my arms. I noticed how the fat around his shoulders had gone away—now they were straight, older looking. And he had a full head of hair now, missing only the sideburns. I stroked him, giving him up reluctantly to James when he came with a big towel. Left alone in the tub, I remembered another bath, long ago, when I had been the child. But I quickly turned my mind to other matters, for it was far easier to touch his little body now than to remember someone else's hand, gentle too and loving, touching mine.

One morning after attending to all the things which needed attention, I played blocks, ball and doctor. Then, unsuccessfully, I tried to make Benjamin play by himself while I read my book. But he would play by himself only if I cleaned. That looked like work to him, and my constant movement somehow reinforced my intention to ignore him.

Preferring to do anything rather than play one more game, I cleaned all afternoon. In the silence of Benjamin's total absorption in his own game, I thought of Marie, working at the cleaning, washing and ironing while three babies played in the playpen. She had not "stayed home with her children." They had stayed home with her as she did her work. We, the middle-class mothers of America, are probably the only grown women who have ever been told to stay home and give all of our energies to caring for one or two children. We do not starch shirts or iron them. We do not cook elaborate meals. Some of us do not even care if our floors shine. So, in order to seem to be engaged in life, we play with our children—for we have been convinced that they require every ounce of our waking energy in order to grow. We pretend that they need us, when it is really we who need them. And we continue to believe the lies we are told about the needs of little children and the instincts of mothers. Who would take care of them if we did not? There are few attractive alternatives. So when we are not playing Tinker Toy or fixing a simple meal, we sit on the couch and watch them, or the television, or the window, and, not even dreaming any more, we stare.

When I finished cleaning it was only four o'clock. Not time for James and my father to return. Not time to start dinner. I placed Benjamin in front of the television, where he would stay as long as I let him, and lying down on the bed behind him, I dozed.

I dreamed I lived in a large apartment. *There are several rooms I never use. These constitute an entire apartment in themselves—living room, kitchen, bathroom. Their presence upsets me, mysteriously threatens the security of the rooms which I do use. I try to ignore them, but I can't help noticing that they are falling into disrepair, growing dirty. Still I try to pretend I can live only in the front rooms.*

I am awakened by the bell. It is James. He asks me how my day has been.

There were two men living in the house with me. Their names were Father and Husband. (James, whom I knew well, had gone away somewhere and came back only occasionally, in the darkness of night, stealing into my bed when everyone was asleep, holding a woman who, every so often, felt alive enough to embrace him. But by morning, James had disappeared again, and Husband had returned.)

Husband was kind. Having spent one year taking care of his child, he was knowledgeable enough to help his wife a great deal on weekends and evenings. He was worried about the woman he loved, who was threatening to become merely themotherofhischildren. So he kept insisting he saw me hiding, beneath the ugly clothes and distant eyes. When Benjamin and I were holding each other or laughing, I came out for a moment and said hello to James. That was how he knew I was there. But in the morning I was either wistful or vacant, and it was Husband to whom I waved good-by.

Husband was smart enough to know that things were wrong. But to the problem of what was wrong, there was no solution. His wife, maddeningly, hated a life which she could not or would not change. Whenever he suggested a baby-sitting agency, she told him about how people come home to find their children murdered in the bathtub by that nice-looking old lady the agency sent over. Every time he talked about housekeepers, she told him about the one who had hit her every day when she was a little girl until she had finally found the courage to tell her father.

"Well, surely there are some kind housekeepers," he said reasonably. "In fact, you were brought up by one kind woman yourself."

"After five mean witches," she answered.

His wife was immobilized, he saw, and there was no solution. Well, he was certainly not going to give up his job which, in addition to everything else, put food in their mouths. The talking stopped, both of them relieved.

Father interfered. He had brought up two girls, an experience which will affect a man one way or another.

"You must find someone to take care of Benjamin while you go back to school," he told his daughter.

Released by that parental command, remembering how he had left each morning and come home each night, I thought, I would rather be a father than a mother.

I told Father and Husband one night what it was like for me. "I cannot leave Benjamin with just anyone, yet I hate this life," I explained. To me, it seemed a very understandable dilemma.

"In one month, I'll be working only part time," said Father, "and I will take care of my grandson two days a week." And he put his arms around me.

Then, as was his usual pattern after having offered something wonderful, he grew angry at the recipient of his sacrifice. Oh, he would never renege—I could count on that—but he spent several hours that night in his room, hiding, burning his fury and fanning the flames.

"What are you angry about?" I asked, knowing it was because I had proved unable to cope with the burdens of everyday life.

What will become of her? he thought as he lay there night after night.

I began to spend my days apartment hunting.

At night I am back in my house with the hidden rooms. I walk into the unused apartment behind the one I am living in. Shocked, I discover that people are living there.

In the world outside my dream, Benjamin cries out in his sleep, and with that cry the dream changes.

I dream that I let him cry too long. When I finally go to get him, he is sick and bleeding from too much crying. He is naked and has lost a lot of weight. He has lost his beautiful curly hair.

Clutching him, I run to the people who live in the back rooms. I tell them to call a doctor. When they leave to make the call, I notice they have decorated the apartment beautifully. Everything is clean. The couch is golden brocade. Then I notice that this is only one of the unused apartments. Behind it is another. I walk in, still carrying Benjamin, and see that it is not kept well. It looks like a furnished room, without personality or character. I am surprised that I have such easy access to these two apartments. But there is a third one which I have never entered. It is dark. I feel there is someone there who can make Benjamin well, perhaps my grandmother who died when I was a girl. I cover him with one of his old baby blankets, hold him close, looking at the dark room.

It was only in retrospect that I saw that summer, lying in between the years in New Haven and the years in New York like a hibernating animal, with any sort of clarity. It had been one of those suspended times when you need to stagnate in your external life so that all of the new things which have begun to root in you can grow in peace for a while, not bothered by still newer demands.

For almost two years now, things had been happening so fast that nothing had been given a chance to settle. I was like a flask of boiling chemicals, threatening always to explode, the glass only a delicately maintained boundary which could burst apart at any moment. There were nights when I still moaned with the memories of the last stage of labor, even now shocked at the consuming pain which, somehow I had believed, could be eliminated by the mighty combination of technological know-how, an amazonian will and a crazy concept of psychological health.

At least I had dispelled some illusions. My obstetrician had whispered a secret to me on a sunny afternoon. I had come to the office prepared with my written list of questions. Why was I feeling nauseated, I asked, and what was all this pain in my thighs? And he had answered wearily, "If you want answers to questions, have a miscarriage, or toxemia, or let something else go wrong with your pregnancy. We don't know anything about normal births." So much for technological know-how.

After pregnancy and labor, the belief in the supremacy of my will had disintegrated like cheaply made cloth which falls apart the moment it is washed. "You can do anything you put your mind to," I heard an old me saying. And I laughed.

And psychic health? That was something you dragged around with you like a ball and chain, which prevented you from lying down on the floor as you wanted to, just lying down and screaming and crying forever, or at least until somewhere in the background you heard a responsible voice say, She has fallen apart. It has defeated her. Put her in a hospital, an excellent one, of course, where she will get the best of care, be listened to, allowed to get well.

Then strong arms would lift you and carry you away to somewhere near the ocean, where breakfast was served every night at eight and dinner each morning with the sunrise: nothing would be ordinary. And several times a day, some kindly person would say, Now, dear, tell me about yourself. When did all this begin?

Instead, the ball and chain pulled on your ankles until they were raw and an adult-sounding voice insisted, Get up, the baby's crying.

I might have enjoyed that summer of routine and silence if I had been sure that it would end, that at some point in the well-organized future, I would heave a sigh and say, Ah, well, I must get back to work.

There were several questions, however, which needed answering before the future could slip neatly into place, pleasantly contained in small notes on a calendar. One question was an immediate and obvious one. Who, since my father could obviously not do it indefinitely, would take care of Benjamin? The other was not to be allowed the full-fledged reality of words just yet; it was not quite time to wonder out loud when I would begin seriously writing again. So I pretended that question did not exist, or had already been answered. Of course, I told myself, I will continue going to school. Any school. Any subject. Anytime and any-where. School is an interesting way of life when you don't absolutely have to support yourself, and you are trying to avoid the complicated responsibilities of commitment. When the girlwoman occasionally would smile sarcastically, I only looked at her in mystified innocence, knowing that she knew that I knew, and that I knew that she knew, and, stubbornly, I remained busily silent.

I was intensely relieved when I moved uptown and began the fall semester. Twice a week I would drag Benjamin, his folding carriage, a bag full of his daily necessities and my books onto the Broadway sub-way, dump everything except my books at my father's house, go to school and return in the afternoon for Benjamin. Those days were exhausting but had a kind of pleasure to them. At night I would not fall asleep at eight from the hypnotic fatigue of inactivity as I had done so often during the summer. Now, though I was tired from carrying Ben-jamin all over Manhattan, it was a reputable sort of weariness. I had worked, spent muscular energy, been out of touch with the inside of my head for wonderful long periods. Getting Benjamin and all his paraphernalia onto the subway required attention. Reading textbooks and writing research papers were activities which were involving, even relaxing, in ways neither writing nor motherhood could ever be for me.

But the study of the customs of other cultures, the conventions of other kinds of everyday life, was more than merely interesting to me. It answered a need not even articulated yet, but nevertheless one that I knew was demanding attention. This area of knowledge was the perfect place for me to search for connections I had lately been unable to make in my own life: there was a polarity I had lived in since becoming a mother which I had not begun to successfully bridge.

As interested as I was in the conventions of other cultures, as excit-ing, ennobling or broadening as those exotic customs seemed, I had always felt completely alienated from the conventions of my own cul-ture. This emotional dichotomy is typical among anthropologists, ad-venturers who are often marginal in their own world. It is their margin-ality, their slight oddness, by which they distinguish themselves. For what most of us view as the definitive nature of reality is viewed by them as merely one possible pattern amidst a score of others. They feel this way initially by temperament, only later by education. They are finally outsiders in both their culture of origin and among the people they temporarily adopt as their own.

I shared this temperament, if not the dedicated interest in the subject matter. And if I always suspected that I would never complete my studies to the point of living in some faraway place, still I was attracted to the field of anthropology. What, I interminably wondered, were the factors which had made me this way?

Had I been shaped by the family and community which proudly defined itself as unconventional, despising most time-honored American truths as bourgeois? Or was I born, with or without the political convictions of the socialist revolutionaries and feminists who were the grownups of my childhood, to an attraction for anything which hinted of rebellion? If I had been placed in a midwestern farmer's house at birth, would I still have been lured by my own irrepressible instincts down the side roads of heresy?

But how could I hope to disentangle the multiple roots of that characteristic which was so familiar and dear to me as being the result of either temperament or education when I couldn't even figure out whether Benjamin was intense and moody because he was born that way or because he had learned to be so from the disposition of his mother who was either embracing him in total sympathy or hurling him ferociously into his crib.

This was precisely the kind of question to which I had decided there was no answer. There was no way, after two months of life, let alone thirty years, of neatly separating the person from the life that created it with every new fraction of a second. Its spirit was hidden from view by the most opaque of shields.

Since becoming a mother, I was more and more resigned to permanent confusion. What astounded me was that despite my own temperament, despite a childhood richly filled with images of female independence—my mother, my aunts, my mother's friends clinging to their unmarried names, their jobs and their domineering pride—I had fallen victim to the most conventional stipulations regarding motherhood. Was convention, after all, so powerful?

When I left my father and Benjamin behind in the mornings, it was not with a feeling that I was going to something unimportant, some manufactured interest which finally was only serving the purpose of getting me away from my child and the house. Rather, I went almost with a sense of mission. I saw those textbooks and records of adventure as bibles, or at least holders of answers to infinite mysteries. I searched for paragraphs about the women and children among the volumes dealing with hunting customs and male puberty rites. I hunted down all the female anthropologists I could find, hoping that some of them had sought out the tribal women, not being content with men's descriptions of a woman's world. There was so much that had been written about the emotional experience and ritualized behavior of new fathers; there was so little which actually described the women who gave birth. But even the little I found described the great pain and profound spiritual changes in such familiar terms that I was greatly relieved. Every moment of identification with women from backgrounds so totally different from my own encouraged me, and as I continued my search, the feeling of the importance of my work grew; it was my survival I was planning.

When I returned to my father's house in the late afternoon, invigorated from the excitement of my day, I was anxious to see Benjamin. Relaxed and calm, I was able to listen to my father's reminiscences about his childhood in Russia, his early days in America, his participation in that contradictory and passionate subculture called leftwing America.

The old face and thin white hair would fade from my sight as we talked. And a robust man would appear before me. Yes. I had been in love with him. It would have been impossible for a daughter not to be. And I would ask the questions which would evoke long answers, ensuring that the romantic stories I had heard a hundred times would be told again. It was not that I really wanted to hear the old tales once more. Rather, they masked for me my father's interminable, insoluble unhappiness, an unhappiness which, almost more than anything else, had constructed the directions of my sympathies and the content of my feelings. It had always been there, or at least since my mother had died. I would hear him singing plaintive love songs in the kitchen as I lay awake hour after hour in my bed. In later years, I would keep going into his room, where he retreated more and more often to his single bed, reading and listening to the radio; I imagined, in the completely unrealistic and arrogant way of a child, that I could tempt him out of his misery with a funny story, a shared secret or a threatening lecture on the psychology of masochism. And our happiness, for there was happiness, was never simple or sufficient or direct, but instead marked always by a sense of poignancy.

"If only your mother were here now," was the inevitable refrain following every joyous occasion.

The only thing which ever worked was discussion of the politics of the past and political criticism of the present. It was not merely that he was nostalgic. He was also interested and well informed. So, as Benjamin sat in his highchair molding pieces of his peanut-butter sandwich into flat pancakes and rolling them into little balls, I would ask my father a question about the Spanish Civil War which had obvious implications for Viet Nam, or his opinion about some new book which had been published trying to establish, once and for all, the innocence of the Rosenbergs. But just as I thought he was beginning to emerge from the despair which always moved around him like a poisonous fog, Benjamin would demand attention, and the old face would reappear. Then we would talk about his forced retirement, his empty days, his solitary nights. I wondered, at such times, who that old man was. He was Benjamin's grandfather. And having nothing much more than that left to him, he was dying.

"I don't feel well," he would tell me occasionally. Well, I thought, he was always complaining.

"So go to a doctor," I would say, shortly, knowing that lately taking any kind of action was beyond him. And swearing I had learned, since becoming a mother, to see my father as a mortal, faulted human being, I continued to pretend that he was invincible.

"Oh, you'll bury me someday," I would mock. And he would look away. I would hurriedly ask about the time he had been jailed and beaten for marching in front of the White House, demanding Social Security. Slowly he would creep back into the present, away from the dangerously empty future, protected by the glorious, brilliant past.

When I returned from school, if Benjamin had been loving that day, my father would be happy. They might have read or played with blocks, but the main thing was that at some point during the day Benjamin had, without being asked, thrown his arms around his grandpa's neck and hugged him tight, saying, "Oh, Grandpa, I love you."

But if Benjamin had cried for me most of the time, refused to kiss the old face, whined and sulked, my father would be bitter. For hidden inside the old face, far beneath the robust, handsome one, was a child not much older than Benjamin who had never relinquished control.

When I turned eighteen, my father had sat me down on the couch, saying it was time for a talk.

"You are a grown-up woman now," he said ominously. And he proceeded to tell me a few things any grownup should know.

"Here is how it really was," he began over and over again, and I swayed with the impact of the blows.

"Here is how it was for me when your mother died. For weeks she refused to see me. She didn't want me to see her that way, she said. So I sat every night on that chair there and wondered what I would do when I was alone.

"Here is how it was when I was unemployed for three years and you children thought I was going out to work every day when, really, I walked the streets for eight hours trying to find a job. One day when they asked for a résumé I was fed up with all the deception and ridiculous lies, so I wrote down on their clean, white, clearly divided form: 'For the last thirty years I have been an organizer for the Communist Party.' Then I tore up the paper and went back to the streets."

"But I thought, but I thought," I said. And he answered, "You were too young to know these things." Clearly, I had suddenly grown old enough to know everything.

"Here is how it was all those lonely nights.

"Here is how it was when the Party fell apart and my life's work dripped down the drain.

"Here is how it was when your sister didn't make the special class in junior high school and all her friends did, and she cried for days.

"Here is how it was when they caught you necking on the roof and you had no mother to advise you."

"But what can I? How can I?" I asked.

"You can listen. Listen when I tell you about how my own mother died, my mother who was once so young and beautiful." At that, the tears would come to his eyes, and he would curse his father who had driven her to her grave with his constant beatings of her and her sons.

Oh, I can see what you're doing, I thought wisely. You don't want two daughters any more. Two is one too many, so you think you'll just make one of them into your mother. Oh no, think you're so slick, I won't do it, I protested futilely.

"You deserve to know the truth now," he threatened, having always done a good job of hiding it.

That was years ago. I had learned, as so many people do, that it was easier than I had thought to be a daughter-mother, and since I had had Benjamin, a motherdaughter-mother. And who was I to be self-righteous? Wasn't Benjamin my fatherson? And my father and I were closer since I had a baby than ever before. Being Benjamin's mother, it was easier to be my father's mother too. Like my grandmother always said, if you're cooking for one, you can always find room for one more.

9

Each morning before school, while Benjamin watched *Sesame Street*, I wrote in my record books. On the days when he was with me I used his nap time to record my dreams. But it seemed so paltry, such a compromise that, hearing the mocking laughter in my head from the real artists, I would stop, ashamed. It is difficult enough to be a woman and a serious artist. But to be a mother too was to deny the lessons of history: the great women writers and the women shamans of non-Western cultures had traditionally been childless. And I was not turning out to be a woman who flew in the face of history.

Also by now I had received my share of rejection slips, terse type-written forms which nicely and politely break your heart. At least by going to school, I could plan to join James in the grown-up world where we would both support our child. In another year I would be in a position to find some moderately interesting teaching position. My problem, then, would be to manage three jobs—one which paid me, writing, and motherhood.

Yet no sooner had I lived with that decision for a day than I would realize I was not satisfied. Perhaps, I would think, I will never find the time and the energy to write seriously again. Perhaps for that one must truly live alone.

When I had lived alone, I had always been slightly anxious about when, at what precise moment, I would see another human being. So instead of doing anything productive, I would rush for the phone, chewing on my cuticles, nervous and jittery until I had arranged a date for the evening or at least the following morning, whereupon I could heave a sigh of relief, certain that this fine aloneness would not become, in the evening, an unwelcome isolation.

Since Benjamin had been born I had no such problems. Whatever solitariness I could arrange was always bordered, sometimes annoyingly but nevertheless securely, by long periods of social, demanding interaction. A few hours would pass and—I must go pick up Benjamin, I would think. Then there would be meals to cook, dishes to wash, pajamas to get out, rooms to straighten and lullabies to be sung. And no matter how much I might have complained, I felt my life to be better that way. For even now those times alone could become oppressive.

"What in the world do you want?" James would ask me, as I continued to examine the contradictions between the woman I had turned into and the woman I might have been. "Perfection?"

"Well, yes, a sort of perfection. A situation where I could comfortably leave my child and then do my work."

Reasonably he would suggest, "Well, finish going to school for now and when you're teaching, you'll be able to find the time to write again."

At which point the carefully tended discussion would be over and the nightly combat would begin.

"Oh, just like that I'm supposed to forget my writing?"

"Then write at night, do it in addition to being in school."

"Let me remind you of all the work I do for the house and Benjamin. I never claimed to be Wonder Woman, you know."

Knowing it to be the most effective weapon he could use against my fragile pride, James would cruelly remind me, "Well, you have to make money eventually. If I'm supposed to learn to be a responsible father from a feminist point of view, I shouldn't be expected to be the sole support of the family."

His point was not only reasonable but obvious. It was just that it sidestepped the complexities of my life so neatly that the confusion I was in only grew more impenetrable. Like most men, James saw questions as things which demanded answers and confusion as an unpleasant state which needed to be eliminated as quickly as possible with easily hit-upon solutions.

But there is a kind of doubt which must be respected for its own sake, a sort of question which does not have an *answer* but which is answered by long discussions about one's feelings, moving deeper and deeper into one's heart, uncovering all sorts of material. Somehow you end by feeling better. You are more clearly understood, you are slowly turning in the direction of change. Often these discussions, so common among women, touch upon something which is apparently unrelated but is the very secret that needed sharing, the one that was pressing so painfully and so invisibly upon your sadness. And although once the connection is exposed it all seems a fortunate accident, that is not the case. Rather, it is the process of quiet, loving, insistent identification, the repeated testifying of one to the other that says, I am the same as you—that unlocks the doors and unravels the tangles. That is what women seek in a friend.

By the time one of our arguments had gone on for several hours, James would be sitting in the chair with his hand over his eyes, which meant, I knew, that he had a tension headache. He might even yawn and, in fact, his body would look more and more tired, and he would say nothing. For what seemed to me an incredibly long time after my outbursts, he would keep silent. I often thought that if I had said nothing, he would not have spoken until the following morning, but would simply have gotten up after a while and gone off to bed.

In the morning he would sometimes admit that perhaps my way was better than his, that when everyone else had been dragged off screaming and frothing at the mouth to the lunatic asylum, I would be waving good-by to them, perfectly sane; that perhaps it was desirable to live every emotion to its limit.

Then I would admit my envy of his ability to experience difficulty without speaking about it interminably, to accept pain without always complaining. I would promise to scream less; he would promise to be more sensitive. And both of us, certain by now that we would not keep our promises, would kiss, apologize and, full of love, go our separate ways.

All around me now, my friends were having babies. Some of the women went back to work immediately. Some stayed home willingly or miserably, not able to leave their children in another's care. Some, being fortunate enough to be trained for jobs which provided part-time work, were better able to combine both aspects of their lives. But whatever solutions they had found to the problem of working, they were all engaged in the same struggles with their husbands. Many couples had already separated because of an inability to come to any sort of understanding, an inability which usually took the form of the husband saying, "I have my work to consider. And when I come home I am too tired for child care. This women's liberation business has nothing to do with me." Some of these men saw themselves as supporters of the women's movement. "I want my wife to work," they would declare proudly, "but she has to work out a child-care arrangement." Mothers were to take on broader responsibilities. And fatherhood—holy and protected and infantile—was to remain the same.

Some women, unable to manage it all, or convinced of their children's need for a parent's care, unwilling to risk the loss of a man, quit all their pursuits and stayed home, either to a moderate enjoyment or an angry self-denial, but usually a mixture of both and always marked by an identification with their husband's career and their child's every moment of development, which grew and grew until the seemingly sudden, apparently shocking, divorce.

The rest of us fought. James's resentment took one of two forms. One was a mixture of forgetfulness and impotence: he would forget his turn to take Benjamin to the pediatrician; he would be suddenly unable to get him off to sleep.

When he felt more forthright he would say, "I can't stand this conflict any more. Do something about it, one thing or the other. Look, I do work hard all day and although I don't mind coming home and taking care of Benjamin, I do mind spending the rest of the evening fighting."

Except that every time I tried to discuss doing one thing or the other with James, we would end up fighting again. I hated it as much as he did, but was equally powerless to stop it.

It was as if we were on two trains, going in opposite directions, yelling at the tops of our lungs into the wind. I began to wonder if the energetic, hopeful, religious pursuit of androgyny was meaningful only in the world of nonparents. More and more when I wanted to talk about my problems with motherhood, which was beginning to mean my problems with life, I sought my women friends. And while I was sad at this step taken away from James, I began to grow stronger without him.

I saw more clearly where we stood; I no longer expected us to be the same. I knew that James loved his child. Yet, here was the difference: I always felt more implicated by everything that happened to Benjamin. The details of his life, the experiences he had, seemed of extreme importance to me. I identified with everything that happened to him, either as the cause of his difficulties or the receiver of his pain. And only in a passing moment—as I watched him sleeping or intruded suddenly into one of his rare solitary games—did I see him as a separate person, neatly distinct from myself. He had, I realized with increasing astonishment as he grew bigger and bigger, *lived inside my body*.

James's body was much the same as it had been three years ago. I was thankful that mine reflected the transformations of parenthood. For these physical changes were an undeniable sign that I had dared a ritualistic passage, and had survived. The fact of motherhood was etched in the marks across my belly, in the flatness of my breasts, in my knowledge of pain.

After one more or less passionate moment, James might have walked away, as men have always done, not bothered any further by the existence of his son. He was a father only by virtue of caring for his child. Benjamin's presence, his demands, his needs created James's paternity. But I, whatever became of Benjamin, even if I had never known him, had become something new. For once, words, thoughts, concepts, abstractions of any sort seemed secondary and even difficult to grasp. For once, my tangible, finite flesh felt like my home. I had begun my parenting in dramatic pain and physical crisis. Like the pubescent boys of tribal societies who submit to the inflicting of facial scars to mark their passing into manhood, I too knew what it was to make spiritual changes physical, to make the abstract concrete. If the customs and rituals of my culture that accompanied this passage were paltry or destructive, even that could not diminish the impact of my experience. For after all of it was done, the moment had been mine alone. My connection to Benjamin was the most fundamental reality of my life.

Sometimes after James and I made love, I would stare past his shoulder, feeling as if something we couldn't grasp was making a mockery of our best intentions. I had not expected that anything could pull me away from him. Loving Benjamin, my father, my sister had hardly been a question of choice, they were almost like extensions of my physical self. But James was one degree removed from all that. Here was someone I had chosen to love, whom I might even stop loving under certain circumstances, who was more a part of my life than life itself. And for that reason he was especially dear to me. For with him more than anyone, I was who I wanted to be.

Benjamin had changed all that. We were mother and father, husband and wife. And although these roles linked us together in familial ties and obligations, there was a danger in them. The more James became "Benjamin's father," the more I wanted him to be the young father I had loved as a child. But he always fell short of that perfect merging, and then I became more identified with Benjamin, seeing James only as an intruder into my perfectly exclusive romance. But the romance was not only with Benjamin, it was also with myself. I was struck by Benjamin's resemblance to me, unable to see any reflection of James in his features. At times the gap between generations would become insignificant; Benjamin would be my father, he would be everything that had gone into creating me, everything that was mine by blood. I felt as if only circumstance had tied our life to James.

It was only when we stood away from Benjamin, when once again our love seemed a matter of choice, a choice which could be rescinded or affirmed, that I knew I wanted to stay with James; it was then I knew that if I abandoned myself to an exclusive dedication to motherhood, sooner or later I would leave him.

For the next few months I immersed myself in studying for my graduate exams, which were scheduled in two months' time. I forgot about permanent solutions and was grateful for my father's willingness to continue taking care of Benjamin two or three days a week. On the other days, I muddled through the playground drama, walked up and down the supermarket aisles, and watched Sesame Street two times a day.

When I felt the beginnings of humiliation or rage, I would try to quell them with assurances that I was no different from anyone else; didn't most people live out their lives in ways vastly different from what they had once dreamed life could be? And comforted by this sort of self-punishing resignation, I ignored the obvious difference between me and those with whom I now sought to identify: the choices I had made did not take me to the farthest corners of possibilities. I had hardly tried anything, let alone everything. And the negation of my desires was not motivated by necessity.

My father, meanwhile, freed now and then from the mask of parenthood, was becoming more and more a friend to me. He began to say things like, "Well, my daughter has always been a difficult, temperamental, but loving person." And he would shrug his shoulders philosophically, smile jauntily and wink at whoever was near. When he noticed my faults that way, seeing them as a part of me and not a freely chosen method of abusing him, I felt acknowledged. And for all the sins of fatherhood, all the real rejections and mere oversights and well-meant abuses—many of which I was daily repeating with my own child—for all of that, I began to forgive him.

We found him one day, lying on the floor in the same room where my mother had died, pale and thin as always, looking as if he were only asleep. The television was on and, since all he ever watched was the eleven-o'clock news, we knew just when he had died.

I ran to him when I arrived, wanting to touch his hand, frightened more than anything else that I would never be able to truly believe in his death, just as for so long I had resisted believing in hers. So I touched his hand and his face and was struck quite immobile by their hard coldness. By the time I walked back into the big kitchen—the room in the middle of the house where he had told all his stories and where once there had always been someone extra for dinner, where Pamela and I had stored our baby peaches, and where Benjamin had hidden in the cupboard for an hour one night before my father had finally found him—by the time I walked out of the little bedroom where he had lived most of his last years, I knew he was gone.

When I called Pamela in California I knew just what to say. I had lived for many years inside her head—and often, grumbling loudly, I had crawled over to make room for her inside my own. For a while, confused by the various interpretations of death around us, we had even shared one head. So I told her knowing voice through the phone, "It's true this time," abruptly writing the ending to our twenty-year-old fantasy.

Then I sat down at the kitchen table, seeming, I thought, quite controlled and crying at a respectable volume, when I looked up and saw two nurses and a doctor who had arrived from somewhere coming toward me with their needles unsheathed and pointing in the direction of my arm. Wondering at their purpose, I turned a bewildered eye to my uncle, and from the other side of the room someone said, "Give her a shot, she's hysterical."

Hysterical? I thought, feeling that the cries I heard coming from me surely could not be too loud to be spent upon a dead and beloved father, knowing that they were my salvation.

"I am not hysterical," I said as clearly as possible and in a very adult-sounding voice, "and I don't want to go to sleep."

But they came closer.

"I don't want to go to sleep," I repeated. "I do not want to be quiet. My father is dead. I want to cry for my father."

But being merely a woman, or perhaps to them even a girl, I do not think my rational tone and modulated voice quality would have convinced them, certain as they were that I required their protection.

Desperate, I began to yell, "James, don't let them do it!" I knew that if I were robbed of these moments by their sleeping potions, it would take me years to find them again.

James, just like the slow-motion playback of a perfect football play, cut them off at the yard line and blocked their weapons with his broad, male shoulder, emphasizing my determination to keep control of the ball.

I wondered why, when a woman is trying to listen to her mind record the moment of her child's birth or her parent's death, do they always try to put her to sleep? Both times, I thought as I watched them back off down the field, succumbing to James's victory, both times I had needed male protection.

When they carried him out, I didn't cry, but only watched him leave that house of sweet, faulted love. Listening closely, I heard the rattling and swishing of ghosts being, finally, released.

Then it was terribly quiet and we left. All the way home in the taxi, as we passed the buildings which were standing just as they had been yesterday, as we rode down the streets which were in their usual order, I wondered, How will I tell Benjamin that Grandpa is dead? I must try not to wail and cry, thinking I will never again be a daughter to anyone.

"I want to be a grownup," I had said, pouting as my grandmother, stern and wrinkled, put me to bed.

"You'll find out someday," she said rattling her false teeth around. "You'll wish you were a child again. Enjoy it while you can."

Oh, I said to whoever was in that taxi with me. So this is what she meant. And watching the world go gray, I stepped behind the curtain and there in the rocking, humming darkness, I waited for the feel of Benjamin.

Part Three
Children

He took his thumb out of his mouth and placed his open hand, its fingers stretching wide, across my breast. "I love you, Mama," he said.

"Love," I said. "Oh love, Anthony, I know."

I held him so and rocked him. I cradled him. I closed my eyes and leaned on his dark head. But the sun in its course emerged from among the water towers of downtown office buildings and suddenly shone white and bright on me. Then through the short fat fingers of my son, interred forever, like a black and white barred king in Alcatraz, my heart lit up in stripes.

GRACE PALEY from "A Subject of Childhood"

The Little Disturbances of Man

10

One morning I was washing the encrusted orange juice out of the bottom of Benjamin's bottle and thinking about freedom. The ordinary idea of freedom was becoming less and less seductive to me. For freedom to do as I pleased meant doing without Benjamin. And that was very simply a tormenting thought.

I squeezed the nipple, the only one he liked any more even though it was flat and fuzzy, and got out the last piece of orange which, all this time, had been stopping up the hole. Still, I thought, flicking the orange pulp into the sink, I am determined to be free. I filled the bottle with apple juice instead and handed it to Benjamin. Then I got us ready for our weekly tour of all the day-care centers on the Upper West Side.

Each week I went back, filling out applications again because they had always lost the ones from the week before. Some of the centers looked nice, decked out in their big yellow rooms with accessories of blue squares and red circles painted on their walls. And there were others—those drab, gray visions you think of when you hear the words *day care*—which I left quickly, feeling sorry for the women who had no better choice.

Some had male teachers with nice bushy beards that Benjamin would have loved or big fuzzy afros he could have nuzzled in while measuring the kinkiness of the kinks which, like most Black children, he had become very adept at distinguishing.

If all the children and all the teachers were Black, I left, making lame excuses. My husband and the rest of his family had warned me that those places might not be the best for Benjamin, light as he was and hybrid. Well, we were too white for most of them. So I began haunting the apartments of older women, usually dried-up and disposed-of mothers who take in lots of little toddlers to help with the food bills and also to bring life into the houses which, after so many years of clutter, seem to constantly verge on the edge of a deathly order. Some of these places were nice, plenty of toys and affection but, after all, too white for us. And I didn't need my husband or his parents to tell me about the dangers for Benjamin of an all-white world with no shadings or nice big patches of brown.

"Aren't there any Black children here?" I asked one lady, a very nice one holding three or four kids on her lap.

"Oh, you just missed one," she said as if I were waiting for a bus. "A lovely Black child, but bright and sweet like yours."

At the sound of the *but*, so as not to speak unpleasantly in front of all those little white children, I stood up and left, letting her know, I hoped, with my suddenly cold voice and icy eyeballs that I thought her a very stupid asshole indeed.

"When am I gonna get a school," cried Benjamin after we left each time. "I wanna school. I want some friends." He knew by this late moment in his life exactly how to make me cry.

"We'll find one, honey," I assured him, fearing that I would have to wait until he was three, another year, to put him for two and one-half measly hours a day in a nursery school, and then wait until he was five to put him in a three-hour kindergarten. By the time he was finally six and happily settled with other children all day, he would be unhappy because of the little desks lined up in a row and he could begin collecting his miserable memories of having to carry a wooden pass whenever he went to piss while on dark winter mornings he developed the necessary wisdom of how to handle muggers.

Not to mention the fact that by that time I would look and feel like a four-times-washed-out Handiwipe. Not knowing precisely who I was, was one thing. But that was a fairly abstract and even superficial question when compared to knowing for sure who I was not. That was a question which could be answered in the present, once and for all and with some exceptions quite satisfactorily. Knowing who I was, on the other hand, had to be tried out again and again and might even reverse itself without much warning. Knowing who I was not was turning out to be an adequate measure for most decisions.

I swore to Benjamin that morning as we began our daily tour of the last schools on my list, that if none of them worked out I would take him to the park where he and I would try to play with strangers.

They were the last on my list and the last I visited. I never saw them again. Then Too White and Not White Enough went to the park and played in the dirty gray and tan sand, threw it all over the black asphalt under the white light of the sun.

One night I received a phone call from a friend who knew about my child-care dilemma and, although she did not yet have children herself, she was miraculously able to take a great leap of consciousness and understand my reluctance to put up with any makeshift sort of solution. Respecting the seriousness of children's problems, not to mention the immobilizing ambivalence of mothers, is a very difficult thing for childless people. Caring enough to actually help is almost unheard of. But this quite marvelous woman called me from her peaceful, orderly life just to tell me that a friend of a friend (a woman who was reputed to be the sort who got things done) was beginning a cooperative day-care center and was looking for members. Not only did she present me with this shimmering piece of news, she even had the date and time of the meeting written down.

I, trying all the while to remain as skeptical and unmoved as I knew it was wise to be, announced my impending liberation to James and danced a pirouette around the living room. Benjamin, who was always delighted to see my extravagance, laughed and grabbed my hands, jumping behind me onto all the tables, rolling over the floor and singing, "Ring-around-a-rosy." He ended his song, as usual in these gay circumstances, with an "Oh, Mommy" chant behind which, by his tone and the extraordinary silver stars in his eyes, I felt such complete love, such forgiveness, such union, that I sang him to sleep for a full hour, peacefully listening to the sound of his sucking on the corroding rubber of his beloved pacifier.

James came home from work by six and so could have gone to the meeting, but I was the one who went. Let James hear it from me, I thought, pointing my nose up in the air and not bothering to button my coat walking up windy Broadway. He had his job to think about. I had my child. Certain things, under the circumstances, ought to be up to me.

When I walked into the living room where about nine women and one man were gathered, I noticed immediately that everyone was white. But not daring to burst my balloon quite yet, I hoped that other considerations might make even that acceptable.

One thing I had decided, I told a well-dressed, confident woman who wondered if we should plan to start prereading activities, one thing I knew for sure was to hell with the prereading, my baby's teacher had to know how to hug.

The young woman who had been hired as the head teacher leaned forward. When she smiled and spoke, stringing her incomplete sentences together, moving her hands around to emphasize her points, I knew she was the right one for the job. When she said she was delighted to be working with a man and assured us that the little boys would be encouraged to play in the doll corner, that was just a bonus.

She almost had me sold all by herself: her body seemed to reach out to hold someone, her hair fell softly into the folds of her loose shirt, and not a crease on her face was left out of her smile. But I had to ask about colors. I pointed out to the other parents that we were all white, which, although they already knew that of course, they might not exactly have noticed. They nodded and affirmed the need and desire for Black and Brown families. The two women who seemed to be in charge stated their concern for integration in no uncertain terms. And for the moment I was satisfied. If Benjamin was to begin his preschool career in a place as white as a little country class in Mississippi, then at least the whites would be the undaunted liberals and radicals of the Upper West Side, who might even be more accepting of Benjamin's racial status than many Blacks would be. I contented myself with the hope that we could recruit additional Black members before opening day.

The next morning Benjamin and I, hanging on to each other for dear life, walked down a dark steep stairway and found ourselves in a dingy gray basement, with no windows and almost no light, which was to be his first school. Two women under the spotlight of a lone bulb were off in the corner feeding white paint to the sandy stone wall. The wall, determined to remain gray, ate the paint for a good hour before the white began to show at last. In the other corner of the cellar, which everyone was referring to as "the other room," someone was painting with bright blue and that aesthetic transformation was going a bit faster. I asked about the back yard, which I had been told was one attraction of the space (another one being that it was rent-free) and was led through the boiler room to a door set high up off the floor. I hoisted Benjamin up before me and grasped his ankle so that, in case we fell, I would at least not lose him in the dark muck behind the boiler. Then I leaped up to the narrow ledge and opened the door. In front of me was a high brick wall.

"It's over the wall," my guide Sarah advised pleasantly. "We have to build a staircase over the wall."

For now we just poked our noses and eyeballs over the top of the wall, and I lifted Benjamin up so he could see too. And there, behind all of that dark gray stone, stretched no less than ten feet of real earth and sand. Between the branches of a big tree there was enough space for the sun or the rain to come streaming in.

"We have to build some climbing equipment and a sandbox," said Sarah. And incredulous at the thought of us doing such a thing, but fending off disbelief, I murmured, "Mmm, hmmm, that shouldn't be hard."

I took a last look at the tree, and Benjamin, using a word he had recently become attached to, said, "Oooooo—isn't it a beautiful meadow?" Then I smiled, trying to appear modest, when Sarah remarked on how articulate and verbal my son was, and I turned to look at her. Her short, blond hair had been recently washed and dried just the way it fell. Her skin was not Cover Girl smooth but, like mine, full of the telltale blemishes and leftover scars of teen-age misery. She stood straight, with her hands in the pockets of her overalls. She was about my weight, not fat, but not skinny either—a fact which endeared her to me immediately. And she looked so certain that this whole ridiculous project was going to work, that a colorful and gay day-care center was going to emerge somehow from that seedy, rotten cellar, that for a minute I believed her.

I walked back into the "main room" and picked up a paintbrush as I noticed Benjamin off in the corner with the other children playing with dust. I tried to concentrate on the painting, but I was really concerned with something else. I was certain that without me keeping a strict eye on him, Benjamin would at any moment begin hitting another child. After over a year of struggle, I had been unsuccessful in stopping his hitting.

"It's part of his general activity," friends would tell me, reminding me of his physical prowess and fearlessness in most strange situations.

"A child who hits is often a child who . . . A child who hits too often might be expressing . . . A child who is overly aggressive is responding to certain feelings in his mother . . . " the child-care books warned me.

"Our children would not have hit at that age. One really good slap on the hands and they learned all right," my husband's parents assured me with never a suspicion about the faultiness of memory.

"Never hit a child," my father had solemnly advised.

But wanting to stop this terrifying behavior before I had to go on to the next paragraph in the book, the one where they advise child therapy, I began to hit Benjamin on the hands.

In New Haven, all the other mothers had said, "Oh, don't hit him. He's just a baby." And for an hour I would agree, wagging my finger and saying, No, no, with the rest. Then Benjamin would attack another toddler with a long shovel and turn proudly toward me, smiling. I was enraged while the other mothers laughed. And I would smack his hands harder than the last time.

I was not comforted by the fact that Benjamin never seemed mean when he hit but only oddly involved with whomever he was hitting.

Nor was I relieved by his equally intense capacity for warmth and physical affection.

All I could think about was my own violence and my own bad mothering and my own shame. But furthest of all from my mind was the thought that Benjamin was a separate person who was emerging with strengths and weaknesses of his own to which I might or might not respond. I just kept thinking of him as a lump of clay, molded by me and taking shape only according to my discretion. I had been thoroughly convinced of the stated and unstated messages which had been beeping at me ever since I had realized there was such a thing as the psychology of child development: with every single broad and subtle, tiny or grand, conscious or unconscious action, mothers create the personalities of their children. And judging myself so harshly, I had begun to stalk the world, on the lookout for the failings of another mother, an inadequacy which I did not possess, a child whose difficulties were blessedly worse than Benjamin's.

Ah ha! I would think as I saw some dependent child clinging to his mother, refusing to let her leave his side. *She* has created his insecurity with her own separation anxiety. *My* child is so independent.

But my competition for the prize of Best Mother of the Year resulted only in intensifying my loneliness.

After I had painted my section of the basement wall for about ten minutes, I heard a child crying. I peeked around and saw Benjamin with that telltale grin of conquest spread across his criminal mouth, standing over a little boy's hunched back and tearful face.

"Benjamin!" I yelled, certain that every other woman in the room was looking at me.

"Don't worry about it," Sarah said. "That's my son he hit. He cries very easily. I'm sure Benjamin didn't hurt him." And she gave her son and Benjamin each his own toy, admonishing Benjamin not to fight and her son not to cry. I knew I'd be lucky if the peace she created lasted for five minutes. So in the moment that it took me to pick up my paintbrush and move back toward the wall, one of those moments when a whole area of knowledge can pass through your mind in a flash though it has taken years to grow into consciousness, I decided to begin this friendship with Sarah, as well as my connection to the day-care center, as honestly as possible. I not only wanted a place for Benjamin to happily spend his days; I also wished, for the first time since I had left Anna and our group behind, to befriend some women with whom I could speak frankly about motherhood.

"Well," I said to Sarah, trying to sound off-the-cuff, at least somewhat less worried than I felt, "I suppose he hits because I hit him too often and started hitting him too early."

"I hit my child sometimes, and he has never been a fighter, so I don't think that has anything to do with it," she said, shrugging her shoulders, answering me in the same casual tone. But I could see in her eyes that she was supporting me and knew exactly what I meant to say.

"The thing is that being a mother is so hard," she continued, and she told me of the series of inadequate babysitters she had used for her two children up until now and why she was so determined to build this day-care center.

"My daughter was such an easy baby," she said, causing a pain of envy to move down my chest. There were such things—easy babies, little chubby sedentary people who sat contentedly in one spot for long periods, who never seemed interested in the coffee cup sitting on the table or the kitchen stove. They were rare, these creatures, the ones who slept through the night at three weeks and whose teeth popped in painlessly, like rabbits out of a magic hat. They were very rare; but they existed. I had seen them. Certainly being the mother of an infant like that had to be a very different experience from mine. Whether these "good babies" created mothers who enjoyed their infants or whether the mothers created the contented infants had once been an unanswerable question for me; increasingly I subscribed to the first explanation.

"You're very lucky," I said to Sarah, sighing.

"But my son Jacob," she continued more intensely, shaking her head and pointing to the little boy Benjamin had hit, "he was totally different. He cried for months and still, at a year and a half, has never slept through the night."

In one year and a half this woman has never slept through the night, I thought horrified.

Another woman, who was painting beside us and listening to the conversation, laughed bitterly.

"I have two children and I haven't slept through the night in four years," she said.

"Jesus Christ!" I gasped, feeling that it would have killed me.

"And my older son was a hitter, like Benjamin," said the tall, thin woman with beautiful blue eyes. Her graying hair hung loosely down her back, thin and shining. Gray hair once meant *an older woman* to me, I thought, fingering my own scattered gray.

Then she looked at me sympathetically and finished, "Don't be too hard on him. I was too hard on my older son, we all are on the first. He'll stop after a while. It's very different with your second," she assured me.

"Oh, I'll never have a second," I stated emphatically. And we began to compare our experiences of giving birth, a conversation which—like a magnet drawing metal pins which were scattered across the floor— drew every woman in that room.

A few had been exhilarated all the way through their comparatively easy labors. And there was absolutely no way of distinguishing them from the rest of us who, until the last moment, had been in tormenting pain. There was, unhappily for scientific conclusions, no way of saying, Ah yes, of course, those women who had an easy time are so much more athletic, or earthy, or healthy, or feminine. Such categories seemed to have no relationship at all to easy labors. I listened to their stories as a joyfully frightened child listens transfixed to *Peter and the Wolf* while he clutches his mother's arm but refuses to have the story stopped. I listened to each one and then I told my story.

"Twenty-four hours of labor," someone said, and we all moaned.

"I pushed until I thought I was ripping apart."

We all laughed loudly, almost hysterically, as we each privately remembered the pain and the wonder of it all.

I looked over at Benjamin, who was miraculously playing quietly with the other children, and I remembered two dark eyes and a pointy chin on a tiny face which seemed to grow out of the blanket roll. His mouth was relaxed in that first moment I held him, and his eyes, although I knew he couldn't see much, seemed to be searching my face, wanting to know me. Certainly I smelled familiar to him, felt like another side of someone he had already known for some time. And I was in another world, a brand-new and quite different world, with the wonder of it. Then I nursed him for the first time and, my slimy inner fluids only recently wiped away from his eyes and off his cheeks, I soaked him again with my tears.

Would that experience ever fade? Would I ever be able to remember it in the pleasant, muted colors of most memories? Would it always, for the rest of my life, pass through me sharply just as if it were happening right then?

"We had better get this painting done. We still have to build the stairway to the back yard today," someone said.

There were meetings every night. There were fees and salaries to be computed; equipment to collect, mend and paint; bank loans to be made. Often I wondered if the school would ever open, it all seemed so insurmountable. But I never encouraged James to go to half the meetings or share the work. I hoarded my joy selfishly, saying I didn't mind the work, meaning I was extremely happy.

Walking home at night, the women inevitably talked about their children, about being a mother. These women were starting a day-care center because they worked already or planned to return to work. Some were desperate for money, others for the pleasures of their private lives. Some of the women were liberal or radical political organizers, a few were artists, four or five were teachers, several worked in offices, and a few were full-time students. They were women who were interested in many things. But here we were together and all we talked about in those early months was motherhood.

We shared the doubts and self-accusations and fears which must be frankly admitted before women who are mothers can stop racing each other to the finish line and become friends. Once the truth is spoken, the women are connected to each other like men who have served together in the same army.

"You don't know about war," men say in their conversations with us, in their tales over a glass of beer.

"You don't know about war," they tell us in their books; "it is very different from what the politicians, the newspapers, the history books and the people at home think it is. It's so different from what you think it is," they say, "that we cannot even describe it to you." And sickened by the recognition of the unhappy and mysterious divisions between fantasy and reality, they are left only with their odd sort of camaraderie, their mocking and hysterical laughter.

Each night before we left each other on the street corner to go home, we touched hands and arranged for the next meeting.

At one nighttime meeting, a neatly dressed blond woman sat opposite me. She worked in business as an administrative assistant, a supervisor of some sort. Whenever I brought up the continuing lack of Black and Brown children she said truthfully that it didn't matter to her one bit whether the center was integrated or not. All she cared about was the center's opening. I argued with her, as did some of the others, but I liked her straightforwardness. I also liked her child—a little girl of Benjamin's age who could hardly speak yet but who loved openly and put her hands all over you. This woman said she had no use for cooperatives, but unfortunately she couldn't find another situation; she hoped she would have to do as little as possible for the school.

Some of us argued that we wanted to be very involved, to get to know each other as well as each other's children.

"No," she said with conviction. She had no desire to know any of us particularly. She just wanted a good place to leave her daughter as she had to return to work, and she would do whatever was necessary to achieve that end. She had problems enough without worrying about some romantic notion of community.

She worked as hard as any of us; the children liked her immensely; she was delighted that her daughter was so close to so many of the other parents.

In a world of expanding permissiveness, she clung to her notions of parental authority. She made the rules in her house, not the children. They ate what she told them to eat and were not permitted to curse. She believed in children religiously washing their hands before eating and going to bed at eight. To me, her daughter did not seem any more repressed or spiritually deadened than any of the other children—only more polite and less annoying.

Just as I had always been attracted to people who were vastly different from myself, I was attracted to her. I spoke to her as often as I could, finding areas, such as early bedtime, upon which we could stand in agreement. I was beginning to learn what it was like to be a businesswoman who loved her children even more than she hated disorder.

Finally Sarah found one more Black child, actually an interracial child living with her white mother. Several Black mothers had come to look at our developing school. But most were not interested when they saw the basement, the lack of adequate bathroom facilities, the chaos. If they were middle-class people, they were not interested in a full day of child care, and certainly not in a place like this one. If they were poor, they couldn't afford the prices we had to charge in order to meet the bills. And we had no hopes of government funding because our basement would never pass the health-code regulations. My attempts to integrate Benjamin's life, even in a neighborhood which was famous for its ethnic complexity, were repeatedly ending in failure. As a white woman, I was finding myself ending up always in a white world. And slowly I was beginning to appreciate the potency of the far-reaching tentacles of racism. There are a Black world and a white world and very rarely do these two overlap.

With two brownish children on the register and no Black parent in the group besides James, we gave up the search. Whether for this reason or for others, James, although continuing to be interested in the progress of the center, never worked on it or came to meetings. Neither, at that time, did any of the other fathers. My attitude toward this was different than it would have been a year before. I did not seek to convince the men to join us—let each woman make her own decision about that. We were all too different from each other to legislate any policy about fathers' involvement in the center. Some women voiced their displeasure at the lack of men around and fought with their husbands to take a greater part. Others said, frankly and crisply, "We just don't live that way. The children are my responsibility and my husband will never be involved."

But whether we were fighting or resigned to traditional roles, the case was the same: the children were basically our responsibility. So let us build and run our school, let us provide for the children, I thought, feeling hostile and proud whenever a man came into the room. When one would come to help with heavy lifting or to take a child home for a nap, the women would visibly change. Even Cathy, my blond, businesswoman friend, became more submissive, ingratiating, unassertive. Surely these women were not all passive and dominated in their homes with their husbands. It was the other women's husbands, the presence of strange men, that had this effect on them. It was not merely the suggestion of a fresh, unfamiliar sexuality. It was a desire to please, to be thought feminine or interesting or beautiful, and there was only one road to that goal—passivity. I felt it too. I had to struggle to speak my mind when men took part in the discussions. Unless pushed to a limit, I tried to agree. I smiled differently and stood straighter. And while the sexuality of it was pleasant, while it was enjoyable to be looked at lustily by a man who had not seen you give birth or scream your guts out huddled on the floor, it was disturbing to have our workplace transformed suddenly into something else. And it was painful to see strong mothers who took care of their children almost all of the time submit to their husbands' will about why the children should not have pizza for lunch or why they should go home now.

"He's playing with nails!" one man yelled at his wife, grabbing his son out of the dirt pile where the children sat.

We all turned away, embarrassed as she apologized for her neglect, bent over to wipe the child's hands, took the large blunt iron nails away and handed the boy to his father. I was thankful he did not spank her behind.

"I don't think you should stay down here with her any longer today," another man advised his wife, who was in the middle of building a Junglegym. "She's starting to cough from the dust."

A young, neatly dressed, gentle-looking father brought his daughter into the school one afternoon and, trying unsuccessfully to speak quietly, said furiously to his wife, "I am going to work. Take your child if that's not too much trouble," and stalked out.

Don't you see we are too busy for your petty interruption! I wanted to scream. But that was precisely what they did see. I preferred it when the men, the fathers, some with their titillating glances, others with their fine-looking hands and rasping voices, stayed away, leaving us in peace.

Two men began to work with us after a few weeks. They took their turns building and then their turns watching the children. Their wives hardly came at all. One of the women worked at a nine-to-five job while her husband was a professor, so he had more time for the child. The other, I discovered later, had gone literally mad after childbirth and infancy had pounded her head to a pulp. He had taken the responsibility of "motherhood" out of necessity. Now that she was better, he still did the balance of the work while she, tentatively, carefully, risked getting to know her child.

I grew comfortable with these two men. The insoluble dilemma of thundering sexuality which one is forbidden to act upon was momentarily controlled by working together; we had something to think about besides attractions which cannot be openly acknowledged anyway. They, like James, knew about getting up in the middle of the night, about the treatment of chicken pox and the price of Pampers. And, holding their noses or simply tolerating the smell of a strange child's shit, like the rest of us they changed the continuously wet or filled diapers.

One morning just before we were planning to open, two representatives from City Day Care Services of the Department of Health came into our school. A neighbor, annoyed by the hammering and building and crying of children, had reported our existence to the authorities. We discovered, to our surprise, that we were part of "the underground day-care movement." Well, we were certainly underground. But we were confident in our gleaming basement. Blue and white walls enclosed play areas filled with dolls, toys, books and pillows. All the equipment was old and patched but to us it seemed beautiful. Covering the bumpy gray stone floor, for softness and color, was a green and blue rug. Doors were red; cubbies were purple. Lights were scattered all over the ceiling. We had built two tables low to the ground since we had no chairs; we had one play stove and sink, three cribs for the babies, and a toilet which was perched high up on the wall, set into a deep crevice in the stone. A bright orange staircase had been built up to it, and when a child sat down on the toilet seat, he might look up above him to a ceiling of contact paper filled with green and yellow flowers. In short, it was beautiful.

Yet, to our shock and dismay, the lady and gentleman from the city agency frowned when they entered the room. They would not close us down immediately, we knew—we had been instructed by more experienced parent cooperatives in the methods of procrastination, of holding them off. But they could harass us out of existence; eventually they could force us to close. The man opened a ruler which looked to be about a mile long. Then he measured every space in the room in every direction, rattling off numbers of inches and feet to the lady, who wrote them all down on a little pad. Every so often she shook her head in consternation and turned to smile condescendingly at us. We stood around her, watching her face for a betrayal of honestly stated opinion. When they were done, she sighed one last time and said, "This is quite impossible, you know. You'll have to find another space, one with windows, high ceilings, a real bathroom."

"There are no such places we can afford and, besides, most landlords won't rent to day-care centers," we said simply, having long ago faced the facts of life.

"Well, children cannot spend their day in a cellar." She finished on a high note and coughed; the children played happily in the huge indoor sandbox, our pride and joy.

We patiently pointed out the window we had blasted out of the wall, the homemade ventilating system we had constructed with two fans, the many toys, the happy children.

"The staircase is extremely dangerous," she said, hardly opening her mouth. The man looked over his figures. Then he asked to see the back yard.

Breathing deeply, Sarah and I, resigned as two convicts walking to the execution, led them through the boiler room. We walked up the cinderblock stairway, warning them to watch their heads as they passed under the low pipes.

"My goodness," was all she said, and he winced.

"Well," said Sarah, indomitable, "the children are much shorter than we are."

We passed through the heavy door, by now knowing better than to point out our homemade staircase as proudly as we would have wished, stretching, as it did, securely over the wall. In front of the wall we had built a sturdy fence, painted orange, which no child could climb or fall over. But they were not impressed.

"If only you could have the first-floor apartments which look out on the back yard," the man said pointlessly, indicating the obviously occupied home of another tenant.

Silence. For fifteen minutes, while they measured the yard and the sandbox and poked at the plastic-covered mattress we had fitted under the Junglegym, silence. All they said was, "Mmm, hmm."

We followed their bent bodies down our red staircase, straightening when we reached the boiler room again, and at last into the relatively open space of the main room.

"Of course," she said carefully, "you do care about your children. We all care about the children." A remark which, considering everything, could not be answered.

"Most people, you know, only choose day care as a last resort," she advised next, and we knew she was noticing the lack of Black and Brown faces. Surely, she was thinking, these obviously middle-class hippies, decked out in their dungarees and horn-rimmed glasses, cannot *need* day care.

"Have you thought of a play group in your homes?"

"We need a full day's care for our children," someone explained.

"We cannot afford housekeepers," another offered.

"We prefer a communal environment," came next.

Someone said, "Our teachers are very loving, you can see." We all pointed at them and they instantly smiled.

"The children will probably be very happy."

We talked on and on, trying to find the magical phrase which would make them leave, and finally someone said, "We'll work on implementing all your suggestions as time goes by and call you for more help soon."

And they left.

That night we decided to open the following morning at eight. The teachers were elated, in love with the children by now and relieved that their jobs were secure. We all congratulated each other and spoke about how wonderful tomorrow would be.

Benjamin jumped around the room, yelling, "I have a school! I have a school!"

I was utterly terrified; tomorrow stretched before me into infinity like deep mourning.

I I

The night creeps around me, coming closer and closer until it is inside my body as well as all through the house. But I am wide awake, my eyes staring ahead, then flashing this way and that. First I pretend that I might sleep tonight, so I keep changing positions, resting my head on my arm, and then, when my shoulder begins to feel paralyzed, I think, If I lie straight as a board on my back with my hands at my side and my eyes closed, I will probably fall asleep. But soon my feet begin to ache in that position and I turn again, this time toward James, who, as usual, is fast asleep. It's not that he doesn't worry or feel anxious about things. But he has this uncanny ability to say, *Now I will go to sleep,* and then he goes to sleep. I think it may be that he *wants* to go to sleep while I, for reasons which remain stubbornly mysterious, want to stay awake.

As a child I would frequently call my father into my room three, four, five times a night, frightened that I could not sleep. Once he told me that if I didn't fall asleep, it was all right, that I might just lie there and rest all night. And this stupendous, liberating realization—that if I stayed awake all night I would not die—became a chant which I demanded of him each time the terror began to inch its way into my stomach again.

"Tell me it doesn't matter," I would command.

"It doesn't matter if you don't fall asleep as long as you relax," he would repeat obediently. Soon I would be asleep.

I lie in my bed listening to the fire engines sirening down Columbus Avenue as I speak the old words: "It doesn't matter if . . . " But that only makes me start crying as I lie there missing him, wishing he, of all people, were at the miraculous other end of a telephone wire. I push his face, which I haven't seen in six months, out of my aching head. Nothing is working tonight. I must want to stay awake for some reason.

What do you want? I ask myself accusingly. Isn't this what you have been wanting for two years? Do you dare to complain, to feel a moment of sadness, of, heaven forbid, loss?

My baby is leaving me tomorrow at nine and he won't be back until four, and the next day and the next day and the next day until Saturday. Perhaps on Wednesday I will make believe he's sick and keep him home, make believe so the teachers won't laugh at me. Will they let me call during the day to check on him? What if he can't sleep on those army cots? What if he hits once too often and a teacher, not loving him as I do, spanks him without that secret silent love which makes the hitting O.K.? What if the experts are right about day care?

This is the first time in many months I have thought of the experts and their theories about the dangers of collective child care for young children. Until this moment I have only despised them. All of us building the center, transforming the basement, loving each other's children have despised them, banished them and their ravings from the relevant world. Now in the middle of the last night of my . . . the last night of something, I'm not sure what, here they come, rising up behind the closet, peeking in my windows, scratching on the glass of my favorite paintings, cackling in the wind. Shit, I think. They are unvanquished.

I get up. Lying down trying to sleep is a torture, but standing up alone in a sleeping house has a pleasant feel to it, and walking to the kitchen to drink something, I am relieved. Then I go where I have wanted to be in the first place, into Benjamin's room.

He almost always sleeps through the night now, after two and a half years, and I can watch him without fear of waking him. He is not in his deepest sleep because I hear him sucking on his pacifier. He draws it into his mouth mightily as he once drew my breast, all night long he finds it and sucks it. In the offices of pediatricians, in the nursery schools I have visited, in the homes of relatives, even on the streets, people have said to me, "He is too old for that." They have clicked their tongues at him, saying cruelly, "What a baby!" But I have told him, "Pay no attention. They are just jealous." And pitying him, small, scared and weak before these stupid giants, I have loudly defended him to their faces, pushing my cub behind me and roaring harshly at them, "Leave him alone. I am his mother and I don't mind." Then we march off together, him sucking that comforting sweet rubber, me remembering my soft, wrinkled thumb. And I am proud having taught him a lesson in defiance.

I sit on his bed and smooth his hair, pull the covers up, kiss him wet and long. Here it is, I think, sighing with relief. Here is the mother-feeling they talk about. It comes when your child is old enough to love you back, when you have known him for a while, when you are no longer physically suffering, when you have grown used to your life's changes, when you have no choice but to love him—more than a puppy you watched being born, more than a roomful of plants you shine fluorescent lights upon each evening, more than a long beautiful poem you have written over and over, adding a word and erasing a thought and finally knowing that the last line must be *that*, that phrase you have been looking for all over the place and finally it comes in a flash and you wonder, later when you read it to a friend, now where did I get that from? You love the child more. I had held my infant hour after anguished hour, worrying, Where are those feelings? And now, here they are at last.

I am soothed. I walk back to the kitchen and touch his lunch box, all ready, then into the living room where I stroke, just once, my desk, wondering. Then I go to sleep.

In the morning I swore to be calm, not wanting to make Benjamin nervous about his first day of school. James made breakfast and we sat with Benjamin while he ate. I dressed him carefully, pulling his shirt on gently. I made his lunch and in the bottom of his lunch box, wrapped in a clean napkin just in case he needed it, I put his pacifier. James was taking him to school because Benjamin usually cried less when James left him places. And at least if he did cry, I wouldn't have to hear it. Then they went out the door together.

I waited for my tears, knowing by now that there was no use counting on reason. But I did not feel at all like crying. Slowly and methodically I straightened the house. Soon the living room, which was also my work room, was clean and neat. The kitchen was sunny and the dishes were washed. The beds were made. I placed my coffee cup on a low table—no two-year-old hands to knock it down. I sat at my desk and began to work.

Hours later I looked up for the first time. The house was still neat and tranquil. No toy rolled beneath my feet. For a moment I thought I heard Benjamin cry, waking up from his nap. Then I smiled to myself and reached out to touch the certain silence. I walked to his room, stared at the emptiness; I was alone.

I called James at work. "Did he cry?" I said in place of hello, holding my breath, prepared for anything.

"Nope," he said laughing, delighted to be able to report the news which, he knew, would allow me to finish my joyous day. "How are you?"

I told him the simple truth: I am wonderful. And I hung up fast in order to move back down the corridors of those big textbooks I was reading and pass through the doorways of my record books until I had returned to my self. I had three more hours to go.

At some point in the day, not marked off as "just before nap," or "after nap," I ate lunch. I looked out the window as I raised each spoonful to my mouth slowly, giving no one bites, relishing the sensual joy of each solitary, isolated movement. Then I drank soda, not fearing that anyone else would want a sip. I breathed and I breathed. I exercised and I stretched.

I watched myself undress in front of the mirror: my face looked the same as I remembered it from always, smallish, tannish, saddish. Straight brown hair. Small nose for a Jew. Dark eyes. Wide mouth. Scars still there from those treacherous teen-age years when skin repeatedly betrays your most intimate feelings, having no respect for your well-deserved privacy.

Now the body, I thought, pulling off my robe. Yes, my breasts were flatter and my nipples were bigger than they had been before Benjamin. If I squeezed them I could still get some milk.

Those breasts have fed a child, I told myself.

That belly has held a child.

That vagina has had a child pass through it.

That body is a woman's, I said, surprised after all these years that it was no longer an eighteen-year-old girl's.

That woman is me. Benjamin's mother. I wonder what happened to the girl?

There she is, dummy, right there in the mirror, I said, mimicking Benjamin's voice as I went back to my desk.

One hour to go. I had been naked long enough, I thought, determined to get serious. Back in my room I dressed very, very slowly. No need to rush. No one will call or cry.

Oh no, I thought, pulling my clothes off again. My bath.

Bathing in hot high water, with no one pulling your pubic hair and saying, Where is your penis, Mommy? knowing that no one will wake up and cry in agony just when your head is under water and you can't hear, bathing in hot high water, lying absolutely still for twenty minutes, is a fine thing to do on an afternoon.

I dressed again, choosing my corduroys and shirt with the care of a princess. Brushing my hair one hundred strokes and sneaking some powder and lipstick out of the bottom drawer, I felt extremely beautiful once more. Time, I sighed. It all takes time, I whispered, posing delectably in the mirror.

Fifteen minutes to go. I left my still neat and orderly apartment and my sweet-smelling day and walked leisurely.

The moment I was outside I began to worry. What if he has been crying half the day, and they haven't called? What if he has had a serious accident and is at this very moment in the hospital? What if . . .

I had begun to walk faster, almost running, wanting to touch him, hold him, feel him.

Accustomed to the steep stairs by now, I didn't break my pace until I stood in the doorway to the room. Twelve children. Benjamin was only one among them. Some played in little groups. One teacher read to three children under the roof of the playhouse we had built. Some ate crackers at a little table. Benjamin and two other children were playing house. He was dressed in a filmy white nightgown which hung long over his jeans. The shoulders draped down over his blue polo shirt, and on his feet were silver high-heeled slippers. Then I heard someone call him, "Benjamin!"

Benjamin. That was his name, his name, not just the word I had decided to call my baby, and for proof of it there it was, written quite elegantly over his cubby.

I knelt down so he could get his arms around my neck when he saw me. And then he was on me, near me again, we were touching and I lifted him up still loving him completely. For I was made strong and secure by the thought of tomorrow.

After about two months of Benjamin going off each morning to the day-care center, after two months of Benjamin loving the center, I finally began to look closely and with some objectivity at the great motherhood lie. My main interest, naturally, was the truth—or, to be less cosmic (for that constant cosmicness about motherhood is what had oppressed me in the first place), it was my own pure, unembellished experience I was after. But first it was the lie, gilt-edged and pearly, shiny as tinsel hanging on a sweet-smelling spruce, I wanted to look at.

The reason I was able to look at it, finally, peacefully, even coldly was that I was sure, after all, that I loved him. But I no longer thought of love as an automatic, biological response; the wine-striped placenta had also lived within me for nine months. Perhaps if I had cleaned it when it slithered out of me, and cared for its pulsing self for two years, I would have loved it. But it went to the garbage pile that night, free of human associations and cultural expectations. It was Benjamin I took home to care for.

Still, there was something to the idea of motherly love. I had seen the hatreds and the fears and the midnight murders fantasied before my astonished maternal eyes. I had hated him and wept for the death of my life. But for two months I had quietly known that I loved him. Before, I had known that he was closer to me than anyone, that I could never abandon him, that to feed him gentle caresses and fruits and vegetables was of primary importance to me. But love? I had not loved him any more than I had always loved myself. In both cases, love had struggled toward definition, had grown out of confusion, knowledge, misery and necessity.

Love aside, for the first time I began to enjoy being a mother. I do not mean the occasional enjoyment and periodic excitement which comes from watching a child grow. I had yelled like a high school cheerleader when Benjamin took his first step. James and I, sitting spellbound in our living room, had stared at Benjamin through our tears as, one evening, he began to tell us something in his usual disassociated phrases and then, suddenly, but with obvious intention and perfect control, he continued his phrase until he had accomplished a whole sentence. His first.

"Today William . . . climbed out of . . . his crib alone and I laughed at him."

Then he breathed deeply and smiled one of the biggest smiles I have ever seen. For, as was clearly his intention, there had been not one "Ah" or "Uh" or other intruder. The sentence had been simply perfect.

And when he made his first pee-pee in the toilet I had felt the milestones gathering behind me.

I call these moments periodic and occasional. Only in retrospect do they gather together in one mass, giving the illusion of long, unified periods of time; so that women will say to you—Ah! but to watch a child grow! Or frightened by your unpleasant descriptions of the early years, they will say, But when she took her first step! When he said his first word! Still, they are really only moments, as separate and occasional as the slight, suggestive snow flurries in October when you are hoping for the blizzard of Christmas eve.

Now for the first time I had found a daily style of mothering which fitted me, a way of living with this new part of myself which felt right, not perhaps worthy of the Good Housekeeping Seal of Approval, but nonetheless right. And perhaps that was all there ever was to it.

I had four and one-half days all day every week to myself, to my work, to my adult friends. And that seemed reasonable, not too much to ask. On the second half of the fifth day, I assisted at the day-care center. All the mothers felt that our presence in the school, continuously and consistently, would be good for the children. I knew it would be good for me. I drew immense satisfaction from my involvement in Benjamin's life. I felt I was caring for my child, providing him with the care I thought was best. Benjamin certainly enjoyed it. Just like all the others, he would jump around the room on my assisting day, singing, "My mommy's turn to assist, my mommy's turn to assist."

Just as the other children loved their mothers, my child loved me. His whirls and twirls and accidental arabesques were curlicues at the end of my triumphal ribbons.

I was struck with the suddenness of the changes in me, the tripled confidence I felt in my ability to be a "good mother" and still live a life which was somewhat similar to the life I had always had in mind. Was it possible, I asked myself, that the simple fact of a good day-care center, a place where Benjamin loved to go every day and which, therefore, freed me from the guilt of leaving him, was the essence of the liberation which I had mistakenly sought in the unraveling of all of my spiritual and emotional tangles? At first it certainly seemed so. I no longer became angry as quickly, my patience greatly increased. So I no longer felt guilty as often, nor searched hour upon hour for the long-buried sources of my anger.

Because Benjamin spent long periods of every day with people we had only just met, I believed them when they told me he seemed to be a normal, contented child. They were not my relatives whose perceptions I distrusted, nor close friends who might tell me anything to quell my fears—they were strangers. They thought he was wonderful, at least ordinary. I had not destroyed him that night when I let him cry for two hours. Nor had that awful spanking I once gave him when he bit through my arm turned him into a demented future criminal. He was ordinary; besides being special and the dearest child in the world, he was blessedly ordinary.

All these things—the time I had to myself, the other children's and teachers' acceptance of Benjamin, the way my experience matched that of the other mothers, the security of my feelings for Benjamin—all of these things enabled me to look the lie squarely in the face and call it what it was.

It had not matched my experience. It had even created some of the more painful parts of my experience. At times it had threatened to destroy me, dangerously loosening the bridle of my sanity. Would I ever be done with it?

The first few months of jubilance passed, of course, leaving me with a changed consciousness, a reminder of total happiness, a sad acceptance of the permanence of struggle. But unlike that other transitory period, the one I had spent in my father's house sweating out the dull, scary summer with Benjamin, this period—like the other one, essentially an interim—was an interim of happiness. And even when it was behind me, no longer adding automatic energy to my mornings and a sense of contentment to my nights, still it had changed me in remarkable ways, the fact that I was beginning to enjoy motherhood being the most remarkable thing of all.

Yet I was not done with the lie, nor would I ever be. Whenever Benjamin seemed discontent, when he fought with the other children excessively, when he cried at being left in the morning, I would think: It is because I leave him too often. And the fact that his moods had varied just as dramatically when he was with me, that he had fought with other children all during the time I stayed home with him, that he often cried when James went to work, leaving him with me, his mother— none of this dissuaded me from the automatic assumption of guilt to which I was bound, and I boarded the downtown subway for school with Benjamin's wails still ringing in my ears, drowning out even the wrenching spasms of the IRT.

Usually on those days, I would end up cutting my classes in the afternoon and racing uptown to get Benjamin early so that he could spend the balance of the day with his precious, essential mother. Of course, when I reached the day-care center at one or two o'clock instead of four, Benjamin would yell at me for coming so early and insist that he was not ready to leave his friends and go home.

When I picked Benjamin up at four, we would often go to the playground together. It was spring and in the middle of the miles of cement, Central Park stretched out endlessly, pink blossoms dotted all over yellow-green trees. Children ran barefoot in and out of the sprinkler; toddlers raced plastic fuschia motorcycles across the concrete while others, content with the four square feet of sand, built cities of mud. The mothers sat on the benches in the sun as long as they could, which was never very long. There was always an injured child to console, a naughty child to reprimand, a whining child to tolerate, an athletic child to plead with as he proudly stood dangerously atop the highest slide in the playground. Very few of the mothers were content. There was no mistaking their boredom, their shortness of temper, their martyred dedication.

"What time is it?" I heard a tired-looking woman ask whoever was standing nearby.

"Quarter after four," answered another, smiling because she knew that behind that simple question desperation waited to be released like a villain in the wings.

Then a third woman said, "Let's use my watch, it has a better time, twenty after."

They all smiled, grateful for each other's support. Nor was I finally separate from them just because Benjamin was taken care of all day. If he was having a bad day, whining from the time I picked him up, it took no more than fifteen minutes, piled as those minutes were upon the hundreds of days and nights, for me to feel the same impatient longing for bedtime. And each sign of impatience on my part drove me into a new sort of guilt. Now that he was in the care of others all day, I could say to myself, You have only been with him an hour. Can't you enjoy him?

One woman approached me one day and asked where I had been during the past weeks. Carefully judging her reactions, I explained about the day-care center.

"How long does he go?" she asked.

"From nine until four," I mumbled, hoping she would misunderstand me and let it go at that.

"My god," she said, not bothering to hide her disapproval. "That's a long day for such a little child." But I could see that she didn't want to discuss it further. Because when I began to explain his contentment and my need for work, she only shook her head with a frightened insistence, furious that I had abandoned a way of life which she considered to have grown out of the soil of immutable necessity. Soon she stared past me, ostensibly watching for her child, and then she walked away. I was left to stand there and watch her return to her bench, where she resumed chatting comfortably with her friends.

What is it? I wondered, vacillating as always between two opposing convictions on this question. Is it that the idea frightens her because it threatens her fragile sense of usefulness, a usefulness which she knows to be pretense? When her days run together as mine so often have done, when she finds herself becoming temperamental and angry during the long winter months when she is locked in her apartment with her child, when her child transgresses every expectation she has ever had about contented, creative, innocent children, does she still manage to believe that she is the best and only person who can care for him, who must care for him if his mental health is to be assured? Which timetable does she subscribe to—at six months old an occasional babysitter, at eighteen months a two-hour play group and at three, four and five years a half-day nursery school or kindergarten? Or is she even more conservative, clinging to her need for nurturing her children for five full years until the state demands separation?

Do the words "day care" conjure up images of Dickensian orphanages where ragged children play in a corner until whipping time? Or do the words mean all those little Black and Hispanic children who troop into the playground every afternoon with their teachers and who, no matter how contented they may in fact be, are the recipients of the pity of all the white middle-class mothers who cover the benches interpreting every cry as a cry of loneliness, every saddened face as longing for a mother?

Pushing a close friend's child on a swing one day, I smiled at the mother pushing her child next to me. Then my friend's child, who knew me very well even at two, said, "Mommy? Mommy?"

"Mommy's at work," I explained, and he continued his cries as he often does when she is standing right before him.

"That's what I hate about baby-sitters," the other woman said delightedly. "The children are so lonely."

The mothers on the bench do not see children from a day care center as possibly happy, healthy children. They see them as abandoned. For if the children are ever unhappy, or want their mothers, which is sooner or later inevitable, this temporarily unmet need is deemed horribly painful, terminally damaging.

Scanning the women in the park, those I knew and those I didn't, those who were obviously discontented and angry and those few who actually seemed to enjoy the life, whose beings seemed to be resting places for patience, understanding and tolerance for the endless demands, I would waver.

They have been convinced of a lot of nonsense, I would think. They are afraid of themselves, have no idea what they would do without their children.

Then I would think, No. They do a hard day's work for which they ought to be paid. They spend years of their lives giving to others, and if that endeavor sometimes leaves them crippled, it also leaves them enhanced, graced with a certain knowledge of human growth and feeling which can be starkly realistic at least as often as it is drenched in illusion. And as often as their sacrifices create the insidious damages which result from martyrdom, they create strong, well-loved men and women prepared to give birth to the next generation. If only those expert mothers might give to many children, more than just their own. Instead, they have been robbed of self-respect by a society which idolizes and damns them, and most recently, by the women's movement too. I vacillated continually between hating them for their cowardice and loving them for their endurance.

More and more frequently, Benjamin didn't cry when we left him. The day-care center was becoming a part of his world. In a room where, in fact, everything belonged to all the children, he was learning ways of sharing which I could never teach him in his room when a friend came to play with his toys. Here, in a place where all the children said good-by to their parents in the morning, he did not have to feel himself deprived in a world of paired-off mothers and children, an odd divorcée amidst intimate lovers. If he did cry when we left him in the morning, I was learning to call the teacher later instead of rushing to him, and she would invariably report that his tears were long dried and he was content.

James was satisfied with the care Benjamin was receiving. But he had never been inclined to the view that the daily routines of a child's life were as consequential as I always assumed them to be.

"He knows we love him, doesn't he?" James would say. "He has clothes, food, a home, friends, He'll be all right."

When all the intellectualizing was said and done, James, the child of a poor family who had not given their children's lives the minute attention we continuously gave ours, still basically believed that we do not *bring* children up, they *grow* up. So that what really made him happy was the tapering off of my anger, the diminishing arguments. And we entered an uneventful, generally calm period in our relationship; a time when we each tended to withdraw, not out of dissatisfaction with the other, but out of a need felt by each of us to regain our own particular sort of strength. We lived quietly for a while, more apart than together, avoiding argument, each seeing the other as irrevocably different but not trying to transform those deep-seated differences into illusory similarities.

James held me in his arms whenever I wept for my father, which was often, but I tried not to burden him with long discussions about my feelings; instead I wrote to Pamela and ran up a hundred-dollar coast-to-coast phone bill. I took the responsibility of the continuing work of helping to administer and maintain the day-care center, allowing the classical paternal aloofness which James had chosen to maintain in this matter to continue. After all, I thought, he shares everything else in Benjamin's life; he does half the housework; he is the best lover I have ever had.

In other words, we let each other be, breathing deeply the perhaps polluted, but nevertheless fragrant, aroma of compromise. And it seemed there was nothing left for me to do but decide to bring my own life into order.

Based on past experience and a resilient faith in the treasures of the inner world, I sought the unconscious night as a place where I might encounter a possible new direction, confirm a still secret awareness of what I had to do next. My bedroom had once been excessively bright in the morning; as soon as the sun rose the rays poured in through the cheap Venetian blinds. So I had hung thick orange and yellow bedspreads from hooks above the windows, which, in place of the draperies I couldn't afford, bestowed total darkness upon me for the balance of the night and in the morning awakened me to a soft golden haze. The darkness, black as was possible this far from winding country roads, fed the late evening roots of my dreams, and each night I lay quietly in my bed, touching some part of James's body for the feel of that exquisitely familiar flesh, preparing myself for sleep.

I stand on an empty beach. The ocean, which I have always loved, rises turbulently before me, the waves, much as I want to swim, will not be still. Then I see my father's bones, dry white and smooth, float out to sea; I stand and watch them, seeing there is nothing left to follow, no one to walk behind. Just the dry white bones which have no awareness of me, however symbolic and full of loss they might seem to my still earthbound vision. I stand and watch them float away, feeling thoroughly abandoned, completely alone. There is a terrible ache in me, then a desperate cry fills the air and I am awake.

On the night before I was to return to school to register for the following semester, I dreamt my father's death.

I run to the apartment after I receive the call which tells me he has been absent from work for three days. I meet James in the hallway exactly as I have done six months before and see the awful truth screaming at me through his eyes, the tense lines down his cheeks. I run into my old house and into my father's bedroom. But this time he isn't there. I begin frantically to search for him, in other rooms, in closets, under furniture. I find him at last in a hall closet which has been jammed shut with an old mahogany bookcase.

I woke up in the golden haze of my room and turned on the lights. Where was that bookcase now, I wondered, knowing it to be the key, for it was my oldest possession. It had been my mother's; then it had been the first one I had owned for my picture books. Where was it now? Then, of course, I saw it, over on the other side of my room, holding all my schoolbooks.

On the way downtown to school later in the morning, I knew, though I hadn't said so out loud, that I was not going to register but to take a leave of absence which, ultimately, would turn into a withdrawal from the doctoral program. But I wasn't thinking of what to say to my teachers on the way downtown on the subway. And when I almost missed my stop, I was not wondering about alternative work possibilities. All those things would fall into place. Instead, I thought only about money.

"A woman must have five hundred pounds a year and a room with a lock on the door if she is to write fiction," the great woman said, and as far as I could see, she was right. All the way through that wonderful account of the history of women and fiction, she was right.

Well, if not a lock on the door, I had an apartment to myself six or seven hours a day, but I had no five hundred pounds a year and no hopes of receiving any portion of it. There was only James and his eight-hour day which every week stretched into forty hours toward a magnificently predictable check on Friday morning.

It was utterly clear to me that at this point money was the crux of my problem. It was a very particular sort of world I lived in; if I didn't make any money, I was not a grownup but a parasite crawling across James's eight-hour day; I was afraid of being left suddenly on my own, trapped in a sordid dependency, losing the self-respect I thought I had accumulated and stored so securely.

A mother goddess cannot make a living. She is merely tolerated in the adult world. I saw now that lack of money was the primary block to committing myself entirely to writing. And whatever others, stronger perhaps or wiser than I, were able to do, I could not manage a job or a lengthy preparation for one and be a mother and still hope to write.

And at that moment, walking as slowly as possible toward Fifth Avenue because I was not quite done with examining my seemingly insoluble difficulties, at that apparently sudden moment, something turned over in me. The same problem, just as complicated as before, appeared to me slightly rearranged, just slightly, like the stones in a kaleidoscope which can be moved undramatically if you turn the sphere only a bit, causing a few of the pink or green pieces of glass to move over and turn around, leaving the pattern essentially the same, but with a new shape of light in the center.

I began to take my desire to write seriously. The romantic vision of success fell away for the time being, along with the restrictive criteria of "serious literary merit" which had always tormented me with fears of frivolity. All this suddenly appeared childish and self-indulgent. And the assumption that art was a regal robe which fell upon your shoulders magically, bestowed upon you as an heir apparent rather than achieved through slinging the pickax across your shoulder every morning and making off to the mine, was revealed as the greatest hinderance of all to artistic work.

Perhaps, I thought for the first time since at eight years old I had begun keeping notebooks, perhaps if I put my mind to it and embark on a schedule of instruction and study, I might learn to write gracefully and have, thus, a means of expressing the ideas I seem to need to push out of my head, so that instead of the continuous hurricanes, some sort of peace might reign in there every so often. Perhaps I can build a simple bridge to that fearsome outside world which, for once, will not be essentially a charade.

Think how good it would be, I said aloud, smiling at the endless cycle of it all, think how good it will be for Benjamin if his mother begins to use some of her energy where it belongs, lightening for him the burden of her too dominating spirit.

But it was a new approach to the money problem which had turned the kaleidoscope. I decided to ask James for a loan which would lapse in a certain specified time period. At the end of that period, if I had no promise of making any money as a writer, I would get a job teaching in high school again, and write or not as my energy allowed. Furthermore, at some time in the future I would owe him the same time period of financial support which he had given me. I was sure James would agree to this proposal. He was confident in me and cared about my happiness. Besides, our life would not actually change. Only the terms of the agreement would alter. By including a promise of repayment from me, these terms would begin to fray the thick cords of dependency that had leashed me since the urine in my Tropicana bottle had registered positive almost four years before. But I was frank enough to realize that only when some of my own money came into our family at last would the cord be altogether broken. Still, it was necessary, after so much time and confusion, to tolerate a period of transitional uncertainty.

I went straight to the registrar's office and withdrew from the program so that I wouldn't have to pay a Maintaining Status fee. I felt a bit weak with the finality of the act as I watched the girl put a little pink clip on my record indicating, Dropped. Quickly I went upstairs to the department office. I felt a sense of elation walking into that office for what I knew would be the last time, an elation which almost immediately changed into nostalgia.

For one thing, I had been inspired by the dedication to self-knowledge which was expressed in non-Western cultures, I had grown as a result of my studies. Secondly, my adviser was a perfect construction of the demanding, rejecting, seductive father, excellent material for anyone's leftover oedipal fantasy. My father had never possessed the perfected manner of dismissing and humiliating women which this man could call upon at a moment's notice. He would look at you over whatever he was reading and listen to your overly intense, obsequious recitation of your brilliant idea for your next paper. When you finished your carefully prepared proposal, he would look back down at his reading matter, make a few notations, read a few more paragraphs, and then look up at you and say, "Well?" as if to question the absurdity of your still sitting there waiting for a comment, leaving you to ask, like a child requesting a pass for the bathroom, "What do you think, Professor?" And he would say, "Fine. Let me know if you need any help," belying the unmistakable message he had given you that he had no time for your silly endeavors, being busy, as he was, with the important work of etching his name in the history of ideas.

On the other hand, he had a very beautiful face. Despite its thinness and the tight elongated mouth, there was a sensitivity in his eyes, or perhaps it was merely pain, which drew me. Me and practically every other woman graduate student in the department. As our teacher, he was inspiring. Cold and cruel to his students, he was passionate and full of love for the people with whom he had lived in worlds far away. And he had a vision of human life as it might be lived, as it had been lived, which grabbed hold of my dreams.

He came to me in my dreams stripped of his anger. He was an incredibly gentle lover or a sympathetic friend. I would meet him in places where I was uncomfortable and afraid, and he would quietly speak to me, clearly drawn to me for precisely the person I was.

In school he seemed to grow meaner and meaner. Whatever clutched at his soul, whatever was slowly building the dungeon in which he lived, was making him so unkind that soon, despite the suggestion of wishful hope in my dreams that there was more to him than that, I began to hate him. I stopped looking for him in the halls. I refrained from discussing academic problems with him. I counted the days until the examinations were over and I could be rid of his presence at last.

On the other hand, I was so attracted to him, so obsessed with him, that all of my energies were magically brought forth to my studies and I was retaining information and concepts like a champion. There is nothing, I have found, which stimulates motivation and achievement like the release of self-destructive sexual energy.

I had not seen him since I had passed my Master's exams. Telling myself I was no longer frightened of him, my hands sweating profusely, I edged into his office. He looked up without saying anything, as he always did.

"I'm dropping out of the program," I said seriously. "After thinking about it very carefully and although I have learned invaluable things here, it's really not for me to continue in academia."

He asked why, being that curious about the reasons for my decisions. And as briefly as I could without seeming aloof, I explained about my desire to write—articles, stories, anything which might have a chance of getting published and earning, thereby, some money for me. I added, clutching my feminist pride like steel armor around my vulnerable heart, that motherhood was almost too much for me when combined with one other major commitment; two had been completely impossible.

He smiled. "In other words," he said more sweetly than I had heard him speak to me before, "you're going home to take care of your child."

"No," I said and started to explain. But he gave me that knowing look which people do when they think they've got you by your illusions, especially if they are sophisticated in the concepts and language of psychoanalysis, and there was no response possible. If I insisted that I was not going home to my child but to learn to be a writer, in fact if I insisted on anything at all, it would be interpreted as defensiveness. If I were silent, I would appear to be vanquished by the weight of the truth.

So, silent but smiling as mysteriously and superciliously as I could manage, I shrugged my shoulders and confidently walked out the door.

My initial plan was to spend several weeks studying the short story. Then I would write my first simple, traditionally structured story with a beginning, a middle and an end. I went right to the library. I had several hours to work before it would be time to pick up Benjamin. And concentrating on the lessons in the art of prose writing which are spelled out so beautifully in Thomas Mann's "Tonio Kröger," Doris Lessing's "A Man and Two Women," Flannery O'Connor's "Everything That Rises Must Converge" and Grace Paley's "A Subject of Childhood," I curled up in the black leather chair in the corner of the library, moving comfortably in my prison suit, which, freed at last from the stiff jailhouse uniformity, was beginning to take on a shape of its own.

Part Four
The Dark Lady

Mazie felt the strange happiness in her mother's
body, happiness that had nought to do with them,
with her; happiness and farness and selfness.

"Fair, fair, with golden hair,
under the willow she's sleeping."

The fingers stroked, spun a web, cocooned Mazie
into happiness and intactness and selfness.

TILLIE OLSEN

from Yonondio from the Thirties

1 2

James had agreed to stay with Benjamin while I checked the baggage and confirmed the flight. A simple division of labor like this one, divided one way instead of the other, had to be an act of will for parents trying to alter their usual roles. For would not the ordinary thing be for the father to handle the arrangements and the mother, eternally, to be taking care of the child? Instead, here I was enjoying a moment of tranquility. Benjamin was still at that stage of life when his tiny accumulation of self-control could, like dry sand in a light wind, blow away in an instant. But perhaps the calm and happy mood he had been in since he realized our California trip was imminent would continue for at least two or three hours of the plane ride; one couldn't reasonably hope for more than that. Other parents, I knew, gave their children sleeping pills on long trips like this one, but although I was tempted, there was something about that chemical solution to the problem which repelled me, and so I prepared to endure.

For the moment my mind was free to wander into fantasies of reunion with Pamela. Pamela—who had at times been my dearest compatriot and my greatest enemy and who was now the only family I had. Especially since my father's death, I had been grateful for Pamela's existence, an existence I had once attempted to snuff out, having gone so far as to fling a long, pointed scissors at her face—fortunately, she'd moved in time so the weapon sailed out the window behind her, merely grazing her eyebrow. That night she held me in bed, patting my back with her small hand, knowing all about my love and accepting my murderous desires, so like her own, as natural. The thought of an extended visit with Pamela after almost a year of separation would have to sustain me through the long cross-country flight.

In the seat across the aisle from us was a woman who was about six or seven months pregnant. I knew immediately that this was her first child from the way she kept looking over in a fascinated way at Benjamin, unable to draw in her intimate smile or her impertinent stare. She was imagining herself some years hence with a child of her own and, no doubt, she was in all ways as unprepared as I had been. She took off her shoes and pressed her feet against the seat in front of her, revealing the swollen insteps; I could almost feel the heat which I knew was burning through her skin. She placed her hands on her belly as it moved slightly up and down, breathing in a more visible manner than the rest of her. There was no way of telling whether her breasts were ordinarily small or large. By the seventh month almost anyone's breasts hang heavily into the loose maternity clothes, and I knew that underneath the cotton folds huge brown nipples lay like two untamed animals waiting for their prey, dripping with expectant saliva. Her blouse was sleeveless and since she was an olive-skinned woman, the darkened spots of pigmentation which come with pregnancy spread out from under her arms into small brown half-moons which sat oddly, as if painted, on her tan skin. Although I was cooled by the air conditioning, she was sweating. Her long hair was slightly matted and sparkling where it met her forehead as if she had been standing out in the morning dew. Her face was ruddy from the deepening skin tones of pregnancy. She didn't seem able to concentrate on her magazines or book. Soon she put them away and closed her eyes.

So I closed mine, and became suddenly aware of a change in me: for the first time since Benjamin's birth I had seen a pregnant woman without feeling sorry for her. It was not that I suddenly was vulnerable again to old, romantic illusions clouding my vision. I saw her obvious weariness which rose from her body like smoke, the blue puffy veins running like swollen rivers down her calves. But more important, I knew what was in store for her in the terribly near future. And having noticed her copy of Thank You, Doctor Lamaze rising like the promise of redemption out of the dark cavern of her purse, I knew she was not prepared for the worst. Still, I felt no pity. I envied her. My belly felt empty, empty as it never would have felt had I never been pregnant before.

I reached out to touch Benjamin's hand but, busily pasting on and peeling off the Colorforms which apparently came with the special family flight, he pushed me away, so separate he imagined himself to be. So I reached across for James's hand instead and he grabbed mine instantly, lovingly, while I thought guiltily of his mother, left behind in New York to worry about plane crashes, car wrecks on the California freeways and all other forms of possible disaster.

For a second I wanted to be pregnant again. Then laughing at myself and my recurring attraction for illusion despite even my own undeniable experience, I opened my eyes, looked purposefully away from my pregnant neighbor and grabbed my pen and notebook. I could count on the Colorforms for at least half an hour. James was buried in his daily indispensable New York Times. Until mealtime I would be left to myself.

"But not if you had a newborn baby," said a voice. I looked up and saw a dark-haired lady standing before me. "Or a year-old baby," she continued, looking me straight in the eye, "or a demanding toddler instead of a three-year-old who is toilet-trained, who no longer uses a bottle, who can sustain up to an hour of independent activity and, most wonderful of all, who is highly developed enough after over a thousand days of life to be able to understand the necessity of waiting, waiting without screaming but silently, for certain desires to be satisfied."

She was the independent woman in me, the woman who lived in a world which had nothing to do with Benjamin.

"You would not be sitting here planning another story," she said. "You would be tired, nervous, holding someone, changing someone, reaching into an enormous plastic bag stuffed with so many diapers and teething rings and clothing changes that you would hardly be able to find the bottle. Or (she kept it up mercilessly, reaching farther back in time) you would be leaning back like your neighbor over there, wanting only to sleep or rest, locked up in the cloudy interior which, as the months pass by, becomes ever more indescribable in words, those dearly beloved sources of your comprehension and security. When you cry, you will not be able to say why; when you laugh slightly too passionately and much too long, that also will be unexplainable."

Then the woman in me who would always be alone, unreachable, invulnerable to friendship or love, tossed her thick black hair and, content with this compelling beginning, she sat down.

In her place stood another woman, less dramatic in all ways than her predecessor. Her coloring was not as dark, but neither was it fair. Her clothes were less flattering. Her face was sadder, older-looking, and her eyes flashed alternately with sympathy and anger. For she believed that of the two women she possessed the greater wisdom, that without her wisdom which was as regular as three meals a day in a domesticated middle-class household, the darker woman would grow thin, lose her energy, possibly her desire, eventually she might even die. And she, this second prizefighter hungry for my soul, had no intention of relinquishing credit where credit was due.

"Being a mother is more than the demanding routines, deeper than the oppressive details," she said with a surprising certainty.

"You cannot speak about the weariness and the dirty diapers and the details rising up from one grain of sand in the morning into an enormous mountain by the time evening has come and pretend that there is nothing more to say. You cannot complain about the sleepless nights and be done with it. What about the sweet rubbing on the nipple that is nursing? the moon-round and delicate buttocks soft as freshly washed hundred-percent cotton? Watch the buttocks change over the weeks and then the months. First there is no difference in color from the tip of the round hind part to the deep hole within the anus. All is of one shade, perfect. Bowels made of light yellow milk slide out like ribbons at first, and the little circular anus, going into a pinhole of darkness, is the same color as all the rest. Then one day constipation comes, enters the world from causes unknown, and for the first time the infant strains, perhaps for hours or even days until, instead of the golden ribbon, tight beads, round and hard, drop out, one two three, and finally a larger bead, almost a ball of it, leaving red rays pointing out from the tiny black sun at the center. The skin around the anus, straining red more often as weeks go by, slowly turns a darker shade of tan or brown than the rest of the sloping buttocks. And you realize that at a certain time in the past, your own body was that smooth, unblemished as the wet sand around the tiny hole near the shore where the clam has burrowed away from you.

"And watch a body which has not one blemish or scratch begin, over the years, to tolerate the intrusion of lesions, dripping blood, skin peeling from the very first ripping off of a Band-Aid—skin that has not up to that point been marred.

"Do you see what I am getting at?" the mother in me, hands defiantly upon her hips, demanded to know.

I knew, but anyway I asked.

She turned her head in annoyance. "My case is not so well put into words as yours," she said to the black-haired beauty waiting her turn out of sight.

I wondered if she would ever say anything more specific, something I could hold on to, instead of the endless metaphors she always flung at me just as if she were saying something clear and comprehensible. Then the dark lady rose up to speak to me again.

"I am not speaking of mere details and practical responsibilities," she said in an uncompromising tone. "It is the effect of those continuous demands on the spirit to which I commend your attention."

She was articulate, this one, strong and domineering, and with great confidence in herself, in her ability to tolerate pain, and I loved her for it. Forgetting I had a child, I sat straight and waited with expectant animation, in silent support, for her to demolish the mother and her incessant poetry.

"Human energy is finite; mental as well as physical energy must be used discreetly, with knowledge and respect. After all of the demands placed upon a parent of young children, how do you expect to have anything left over for more than a superficial sort of involvement in other aspects of life? I am speaking of the terrible vulnerability which drags you daily, weary and defeated, down the road to every evening's enervation. Have you not feared one thousand times that you have been a bad mother? And is that feeling not infinitely more painful than the fear that you have written an inelegant story or received a low mark on your last examination? Is not the sense of culpability so overwhelming that you seek sleep, finally only sleep, for sustenance?

"I have watched all you mothers turn your minds to those disgusting everlasting details, talking, talking, talking about your little methods, comparing one to the other over and over, boring the very breezes which would hope to refrain from entering your windows. Yet I have known that it was not the little trick of soaking a pacifier in honey for a colicky baby that claimed your attention; nor even the delicate balance of sternness and gentleness which must be achieved in order for toilet training to proceed smoothly that really interested you. It was the desperate reaching for a moment of confidence you were after.

"Confidence is destroyed by motherhood. Sooner or later the child disappoints you, perhaps even terrifies you with a small sign of distorted development or a subtle betrayal of temperamental weakness. And that repeated death and resurrection of confidence which daily besieges you ultimately cripples the proud and brilliant prima donna in you until she can dance no more. What are you left with?" the dark lady asked in the tone of a sympathetic mother who knows she must be harsh and realistic for your own good.

"Face it. When you have children you sacrifice the full promise of your potential. Everything becomes a compromise, and the more children you have, the more deadly becomes the destruction of your independent soul."

She backed off with a majestic assurance. But I, having been convinced by the merits of her arguments, was left dazed. I sank into my seat, knowing she was right about everything, and looked disdainfully at the mother who, apparently unwounded, was coming toward me again.

"Once upon a time," she began in the unwavering and controlled voice of an experienced actress, "there was a newborn baby. It was clear to all who saw him that he could not walk or talk or even put his finger in his mouth when he wanted to. He had to be turned over by someone else, dressed by someone else, fed by someone else. All these things were obvious. But there were other inabilities which were less obvious to the eye of a casual visitor or even a frequently present friend. Only those who cared for him every single day and night noticed that he had no sense of himself. At times he responded to his parents' bodies and to the fuzzy blanket with equal passion. And when he drank from his mother's breast or the bottle which his father lovingly fed him, his parents wondered if he knew that the rest of their bodies were attached to the milk-giving part which he demanded so regularly. Or was it just the warm milk dripping through the supple nipple that he loved as he nuzzled against something soft? Or did he love at all? Did he know that in spite of all the anger he was supremely valued by them so that someday he would see himself as valuable? That, you see, is what his parents wanted for him most of all."

I moved around in my seat. Stories. Stories and metaphors were all I ever got from this one. But she proceeded, ignoring my clear impatience.

"The years passed, leaving the parents changed, exhausted and resigned to the limitations of life. And then one day, when he was about four, they overheard the following conversation between their child and a visitor who had come to their house for dinner.

" 'You are a rough little one,' said the visitor, who did not intend to be insulting, but only to remark on the wildness with which the child tore through the house creating mayhem as he went.

" 'So what?' retorted the child, less politely than his parents would have wished. 'That's the way I am. I don't have to be like everyone else you know.'

"Impressed because she loved the child and was glad to see the development of self-confidence, the visitor laughed appreciatively and said, 'You know you're beautiful?'

" 'I know,' answered the child unpretentiously.

"At that, remembering the mysterious creature who had lain in their arms drinking warm milk, that little animal who stubbornly hoarded the secrets of his soul and gave them no encouragement for so long a time, who allowed them to stagger forward blindly, praying to god that they were at least occasionally doing the right thing, the parents each betrayed a very impertinent look of pride. That night they made transcendent love and slept soundly."

I had to admit she had made her point. I was no longer slouching in my seat. Instead I felt a sense of accomplishment.

"Satisfaction is the enemy of creativity," warned the dark lady, walking up next to the mother in broad strides. "Domestic life deafens you to the messages from the inner world which alone can nourish a vital, productive person. After all, what is conventionality? It is the worshiping of evenness, the fear of intensity, the demand for emotional predictability— the very things we are told make the best environment for developing children. That is why great women have so rarely been mothers."

"You are romantic and sentimental," the mother interrupted, pointing at the dark lady in an accusatory manner. "A mother can be any sort of person, great or ordinary, given to moderation or intensity, inclined toward amazonian aggression or receptivity. But whatever type you are, being a mother forces you to accept your limitations. And when you accept your limitations as a mother, you begin to accept your limitations in other areas of life as well. The daily grinding friction of motherhood will give you the chance, at least, of relinquishing some of your egotism. You will finally cease to be a child. And grownups see a world which, although less colorful, promising and uniformly dazzling than the child's, is also more pitiable and proportioned. The giants of your childhood shrink to normal size. The fairy tales acquire their share of unhappy endings. Even your once omnipotently evil parents seem deserving of pity now."

But the dark lady said, "Retaining the childlike view of the world, avoiding that pedestrian outlook is the magic I live on. Having one child has all but dissipated the possibility of adventure and innocence. Any more will do me in."

"Stop being so selfish and dramatic," said the mother. "Benjamin needs a brother or a sister."

I stared at her. The words hung in the air, turning the succulent feast of reasonable dialogue into easily digestible pablum. Was this, then, the point of the argument? I looked at both women in startled outrage. Were we back to my pregnant neighbor and the surely transitory feelings she had called forth in me?

"The mother knot has got you," the mother almost hissed at me. "Don't you want the feeling of a baby moving inside you again? Don't you want the incomparable moment of excruciating pain opening up into a new life again? The other worldliness of the early weeks again, the feeding from your body? Knowing how soon he will move away from you, it will be all the more precious. How would you feel now if you didn't have Pamela? Benjamin needs a sibling."

"It will kill me," warned the dark lady. "I can only bear so much. I want to live freely and with great energy. I want to feed on spices and wine, not milk and potatoes."

I reached out for her hand guiltily, as you would to touch a favorite child, pitying her because you fear you will always love her best.

"Pay no attention to her," said the mother. "She's not as delicate as she would like you to believe. She'll always be there waiting."

Again? I asked them both. The pain and the torment again? The long months of withdrawal, the undersea adventure with not enough oxygen, the slow submerging into a world away from the world, deeper and deeper as the months go by until it is finally born and you reach the deepest and most faraway level of all, fathoms away from ordinary life, a two- or three-year swim away?

"I will help you with the pain, I am used to it," said a voice which I assumed to be the mother's. But when I looked up it was the dark lady who was speaking. She was looking at me kindly and then she did a shocking thing. She began to pull on the skin of her face; she stretched it this way and that, until I realized it was nothing but a well-made mask all along. The fit had been perfect. The impersonation had been totally convincing; but an impersonation it most assuredly was, because the mask was coming off, the lustrous dark hair with it and, standing before me, sweating and weak from her performance, was the mother. I hardly needed to look over to where the mother had been standing, for I knew now what they had been up to. But not wishing to rob them of their final curtain I looked, and *where the mother had been, holding a wrinkled mask with straight brown hair in her hand, stood the dark lady.*

Nearing San Francisco, I tried to hold tightly to the surface of my mind, the part nearest my eyes which struggled to see the Grand Canyon out the window, believing it to be there on pure trust; the pilot had said it was there.

I looked ahead again, concentrating on Pamela's grown-up face, obliterating the little girl clinging to me, crying because she could no longer remember what her mother looked like. She asked me if I could be her mommy. I laughed bitterly, even at nine, to think that at such an age all this should be expected of me. But I said yes.

Trying to forbid any intruding associations to interfere with my simple, concrete thoughts, I locked my eyes on the red exit sign so they would not turn inward: the trip has gone surprisingly smoothly; Benjamin has slept, eaten, even watched the movie with James. Only now in the last hour is he beginning to whine.

"When will we be there?" he said forty-nine times in the next half hour.

Well, that was forgivable. I had done that.

"I want to see Pamela right now," he said absurdly. My friend Peter who had no children would have said, "Now Benjamin, think about it. Is what you're asking for possible? Here we are way up in the sky and Pamela is way down there, how can we . . . ," having very little understanding that children often do not talk from the surface level.

I want to see Pamela right now, said my deeper mind.

The pregnant woman got up and paced the plane. Up the aisle she went, slowly, like the baby's father in the old stories, waiting for the doctor to come out saying congratulations, it's a . . . and the man, smoking a cigarette, exhales proudly and goes to the window to see . . . my father had told me that's how it was.

Then she came back down toward me seeming to say, It's almost over now for us, for you and that patient child of yours and for me and my sore belly. Almost over and time for it to come out.

What was the beauty I kept noticing in her face, what was the graceless majesty of her stride?

I no longer worship her, I thought. I don't pretend that she is happy or fulfilled. I know only that she continues. Over the years, *the years*, she will learn to express love when she feels only hatred and fatigue. Soon these emotions will not be so peculiarly distinct. In the middle of the four hundredth dark night, for a passing moment not meant to last, there will suddenly be only a hand which has learned to stroke rhythmically, just a hand touching childish skin; the love is in the fingers; the anger that bores holes in the heart for the moment will not harm the child.

How can I say she is a queen or even a four-star general? She is only a foot soldier. Killing and being killed. Deserting and dying a hero. Nothing but the blood is certain. A foot soldier lost to her unit. How can I enshrine her, all filthy and covered with grime?

"But," people will say, "she is the mother of our children, the next generation, the future of the world!" Trumpets will blast.

Yes, I answer, pulling my cap rakishly over my forehead; there is a wicked look in my eye, a sly grin covering my muddy face as I parade before them. Yes, I see the children. They are blinding me. They dance a circle of ropes around me, tying my arms to my belly while you sit in the spectator's box, applauding. Don't you dare point out the children to me, not unless they have shit their golden ribbons and their smelly green colicky balls into your dishpan hands. Not until your dreams have flown out the window one thousand times do you earn the right to make speeches in my honor. Only when you have made so many mistakes that you see your name on the list of Killers of Broken Children right next to mine. The only other meaningful alternative is separate houses. You in yours. The children in mine.

In the last fifteen minutes of descending, strapped to our lonely seat belts, Benjamin and I held hands. He kept looking over at me, smiling the expectant, excited smile we both used for special occasions. There was no need for words with him.

James too was looking at me with a grin which said, I know we're scared, what are we doing up in the sky? and he fingered Benjamin's fingers. I spent a few minutes planning how to quickly unlock all the belts if we dove into flames so that we could die hugging. Once I had that figured out I relaxed a little.

"Mommy, do you love Pamela better than you love me?" asked Benjamin on the way down.

"I love you differently," I answered, thankful that some things were still automatic.

"But who do you love more?" he said.

"Benjamin, you can't measure these things," I said abruptly, but Benjamin didn't understand the word "measure."

"I love you eighty-four," he explained with a shrug of confidence, wondering why things which seemed so simple to him were beyond his mother's intelligence.

"I love you eighty-four too," I agreed, falling into the trap.

"Then how much do you love Pamela and Daddy?" he asked and James snickered.

"How much do you love me?" I asked James.

"Eighty-four," he answered.

"How much did you love me before we had Benjamin?"

"About fifty or fifty-one," he said.

James, brother, cellmate, companion, sturdy survivor of the death of romance, can we stand another one?

"Mommy!" said Benjamin sternly, waiting for an answer.

"I love Pamela eighty-four in a sister way and Daddy eighty-four in a husband way," I said, praying that would be that.

"How much do you love Grandma and Uncle Ricky and Joan and Mr. Carter who lives next door to Maria?"

Sighing, I capitulated to the need for definiteness. "Sixty, sixty, fifty-seven, and I don't love Mr. Carter at all, I only like him. Look at the lights, Benjamin."

We all peered out together at the dark city.

"There she is!" yelled Benjamin, but only thousands of yellow lights welcomed us.

Well, old girl, he would have said had he been here now, just a couple more minutes and we'll be seeing your sister again. He would be wanting me to act excited for him, but his cheeks would be reddening at the thought of being with both his daughters again.

"Well, Benjamin," I said, reddening, "in a few minutes we'll see Aunt Pamela."

And frozen to my grown-up ground, I watched him jump up and down on the seat, attracting everyone's attention, laughing wildly.

The pregnant woman packed her bags, combed her hair and looked in my direction to smile good-by. I nodded respectfully and saluted.

Library of Congress Cataloging-in-Publication Data

Lazarre, Jane.

The mother knot / Jane Lazarre : introduction by Maureen T. Reddy.

Originally published: New York : McGraw-Hill, c1976.

ISBN 0-8223-2039-8 (pbk. : alk. paper)

1. Lazarre, Jane.   2. Mothers—United States—Biography.

3. Motherhood—United States.   4. Mother and child—United States.

I. Reddy, Maureen T.   II. Title.

HQ759.L38 1997

306.874'3—dc21   97-13516 CIP